WALES
and
BRITAIN

1906 - 1951

ROGER TURVEY

Hodder & Stoughton
A MEMBER OF THE HODDER HEADLINE GROUP

Acknowledgements

The cover illustration has been provided courtesy of the Trustees of the Imperial War Museum.

The Publishers would like to thank the following for permission to reproduce material in this volume:
BBC Radio for a quote taken from Radio 4; The BMJ Publishing Group for an extract from the *British Medical Journal* (1946); Carcanet for an extract from *Goodbye to All That* by Robert Graves (1929); Cardiff City Council for an extract from the City of Cardiff tourist information leaflet; The Daily Mail for an extract from the *Daily Mail* (1948); David and Charles for an extract from *Wales: The Shaping of a Nation* by Prys Morgan and David Thomas (1984); ESIS, Wales for an extract from *The Experiences of Wales in the Depression* (1986); Gomer Press for extracts from *Welsh Nation Builders* by Gwynfor Evans (1988), *Coal Society* by David Egan (1987) and *People, Protest and Politics: Case Studies in Twentieth-Century Wales* by Gareth E Jones (1987); Victor Gollancz for an extract from *The Problem of Distressed Areas* by Wal Harrington (1937); Heinemann Educational Books for an extract from *Britain and the Modern World* (1969); Peter Lane for an extract from British History: 1750 to the Present Day; Longman for an extract from *A History of the Twentieth Century* by Bryn Callaghan (1987); Mr Gywn Morris and Mr Ceinfryn Morris for an extract from *The Angry Summer* by Idris Davies (1943); MSI for an extract from the *Daily Mirror* (1940); Penguin for extracts from *Britain in the Modern World: The Twentieth Century* by E Nash and A Newth (1967) and *The First Day of the Somme* by N Middlebrook (1971); The National Museum of Wales for an extract from *Coal's Domain* (1993); The Observer for an extract from *The Observer* (1951); extracts from *Rebirth of a Nation: Wales 1880-1980* by Kenneth Morgan (1981), *Lark Rise to Candleford* by Flora Thompson (1939) and *English History 1914-15* by AJP Taylor (1965) by permission of Oxford University Press; the South Wales Evening Post for an extract from *Memories of Swansea at War* (1988); the New Statesman for an extract from the *New Statesman and Nation Magazine* (1935); University of Wales Press for an extract from 'The Move from the Land' by John Williams in *Wales 1880-1914* by GE Jones (1988); Virago Press for an extract from *Round about a Pound a Week* by Mrs Pember Reeves (1913).

The Publishers would like to thank the following for permission to reproduce copyright illustrations in this volume:
Mary Evans Picture Library 7A, 28A, 29B; Mansell Collection 7B, 12E, 14A, 15B, 20E, 24B, 67B, 68E, 89G, 108A, 118A, 153F; British Library of Political and Economic Science (Coll Misc 519/90) 9B, (Coll Misc 519/31) 9C; Hulton Getty 9, 13J, 17E, 22, 26A, 57H, 66, 86D, 98B, 99D, 115, 120A, 133D, 136C, 147B; Museum of Welsh Life 12G, 49E, 73D; The Centre for the Study of Cartoons and Caricature 19A, 64A; The British Library Newspaper Library 21, 31C, 31D, 46C, 71B, 102A, 105F, 119F, 131B, 135B, 136D, 141B, 143A, 144B; The National Museum of Labour History 27B, 44B, 154, 159B; Museum of London 30A; Gwynedd Archives Service 32, 69, 104D; Welsh Industrial and Maritime Museum 36A, 157E; Neil Jones 39D, 39E, 39F, 155B; Glamorgan Record Office 45D, 97I; National Library of Wales 49C, 74A, 77C, 123B; John Frost Newspapers 52A, 145C, 148A; Imperial War Museum, London 51C, 53B, 54E, 55H, 58B, 60A, 61B(b), 63C(r), 65C, 65D, 127C, 127D, 132A, 134A, 137F; The Kobal Collection 58A; Public Record Office 61B(t); Peter Newark's Military Pictures 63C(l), 137G; Commonwealth War Graves Commission 75F; Corbis UK Limited 81B; Electricity Association 87F; Topham Picturepoint 91B, 94F; Express Newspapers plc 94E,; South Wales Coalfield Collection, University of Wales Swansea Library (SWCC: POS) 95B, (SWCC: PHO/DIS/56) 96C; Aquarius 107C; Denis Gifford Collection 107D; Solo/Centre for the Study of Cartoons and Caricature 111A, 113C, 118B, 118C, 119D, 151D; Popperfoto 138H, 140, 147A, 155C, 157D; Express Newspapers plc/Centre for the Study of Cartoons and Caricature 131C; Punch 151E; South Wales Evening Post 132 B, 133 E.

Every effort has been made to trace and acknowledge ownership of copyright. The publishers will be glad to make suitable arrangements with any copyright holders whom it has not been possible to contact.

A Note on Abbreviations
Please note that s. has been used as an abbreviation for shillings and d. has been used as an abbreviation for old pence.

British Library Cataloguing in Publication Data

A catalogue record for this title is available from The British Library

ISBN 0 3406 79719

First published 1997
Impression number   10 9 8 7 6 5 4 3 2 1
Year   2002   2001   2000   1999   1998   1997

This book is published with the financial support of the Curriculum and Assessment Authority for Wales (ACAC).

AWDURDOD CWRICWLWM AC ASESU CYMRU
CURRICULUM AND ASSESSMENT AUTHORITY FOR WALES
ACAC

Typeset by The University of Wales, Aberystwyth, Wales
Printed in Great Britain for Hodder & Stoughton Educational, a division of Hodder Headline Plc,
338 Euston Road, London NW1 3BH by Cambridge University Press.

Contents

The Edwardian Era and the First World War 1906–1919

Unit 1: Pre-War Politics 6

Unit 2: Economic Developments 32

Unit 3: The First World War 50

Unit 4: Social, Cultural and Religious Change 72

Depression, War and Recovery 1930–1951

Unit 1: Life in the Depression 84

Unit 2: Britain and the Threat of Germany 108

Unit 3: War on the Home Front 126

Unit 4: Post-War Wales and England 142

Glossary 160

Index

The Edwardian Era
AND THE
First World War
1906–1919

UNIT 1: PRE-WAR POLITICS
Key Issue: *To what extent was there a demand and a need for social and political reform in the period 1906–14?*

The Dawn of a New Century:
Wales and England in 1900 6

Liberals and Conservatives:
Edwardian Politics and the Election of 1906 8

Poverty and the Poor:
Edwardian Society in Crisis? 10

'New' Liberalism and the
Liberal Social Reforms, 1906–14 14

Democracy in Crisis?
The 'People's Budget' of 1909 18

The Rise of Labour 22

Profile: Keir Hardie 26

'A woman's place...?'
The Suffragette Movement 28

Focus: Emily Davison and the 1913 Derby 30

UNIT 2: ECONOMIC DEVELOPMENTS
Key Issue: *1906–14: The golden age of Welsh heavy industry?*

Wales in Industrial Britain 32

King Coal 36

The Development of Cardiff 38

Profile: D.A. Thomas 40

Trade Unions and Industrial Unrest 42

Focus: Tonypandy, 1910 46

Rural Wales: Transition and Change 48

UNIT 3: THE FIRST WORLD WAR
Key Issue: *What were the effects of the First World War on the people?*

The Great War, 1914–18 50

Recruitment, Conscription and Objection 52

Focus: Wales and the Western Front 56

Britons at War: Life in the Trenches 58

The Impact of War on Civilian Life 60

'The war to end all wars':
A Welshman at the Paris Peace Conference 64

Profile: David Lloyd George 66

'A land fit for heroes': Britain 1919–22 70

UNIT 4: SOCIAL, CULTURAL AND RELIGIOUS CHANGE
Key Issue: *How and why did people's attitudes and values change in the period 1906–19?*

Wales – Language and Identity 72

Profile: Hedd Wyn and the War Poets 74

Church and Chapel:
The Religion of the People 76

'Opportunities for all': State Education 78

Popular Entertainment .80

1906	Liberals defeat Conservatives in general election. Henry Campbell-Bannerman becomes Prime Minister. The ILP becomes the Labour Party.
1908	Campbell-Bannerman resigns. Herbert Asquith becomes leader of the Liberal Party and Prime Minister. David Lloyd George becomes Chancellor of the Exchequer.
1909	Lloyd George introduces 'The People's Budget'. Old age pensions and unemployment insurance schemes are introduced for the first time.
1910	King Edward VII dies. George V crowned King. Tonypandy riots.
1911	Industrial unrest leads to strikes across the country.
1913	A leading member of the Suffragette movement, Emily Davison, is killed by the King's horse at the Derby.
1914	Outbreak of the First World War.
1915	Keir Hardie, MP for Merthyr Tydfil and founder of the Labour movement, dies.
1916	Battle of the Somme begins. Lloyd George succeeds Asquith as Prime Minister. Liberal Party splits.
1917	The USA enters the war. The Russian Revolution forces Russia out of the war. Lenin becomes leader of the first communist government in history.
1918	The First World War ends in defeat for Germany and her allies. Coupon Election. Lloyd George elected Prime Minister of a coalition government. Women aged 30 given the vote. First woman MP elected to the House of Commons.
1919	Treaty of Versailles signed. Royal Commission on coal industry recommends nationalisation of the industry.
1920	Disestablishment of the Church in Wales. British Communist Party founded.

PRE-WAR POLITICS

The Dawn of a New Century: Wales and England in 1900

> **KEY ISSUE:**
> *To what extent was there a demand and a need for social and political reform in the period 1906–14?*

In 1900 Wales formed a very small part of the vast British Empire which stretched across nearly a quarter of the world's surface. The British Empire was wealthy and powerful and it had the largest and most modern navy in the world to protect it. The centre of that Empire was London, the largest city in the world with a population of over 6 million people.

The industrial revolution of the eighteenth and nineteenth centuries had made Britain the 'workshop of the world'. It had become a country of large cities, thriving markets and busy ports exporting her wealth to the world and importing raw materials from its colonies. Much of Britain's industrial power and economic wealth came from Wales, a land of coal mines, slate quarries, iron and steel industries.

Britain was admired and respected particularly for its institutions of government, law and the monarchy. Queen Victoria had ruled the country for over 60 years since 1837 and as a result of a large family and a series of marriages was related to many other royal families in Europe. Her eldest son Edward was Prince of Wales and both he and the rest of the royal family were very popular. Unlike some of her **autocratic** kingly relatives in countries like Germany and Russia, Victoria governed in name only. Britain was a **democracy** and the centre of its political power was the Houses of Parliament. The House of Commons was made up of the elected representatives of the various political parties. The two most powerful were the Conservatives and the Liberals. Members of the House of Lords, however, were not elected. They took their seats by privilege of birth and title.

The nineteenth century had witnessed massive political changes. The most important of these was the extension of the right to vote. The last of the great Parliamentary Reform Acts in 1884 had **enfranchised** all male householders, many of whom came from the working classes. But women were still denied the right to vote.

New Challenges

The new century brought fresh challenges. Britain faced competition from emerging industrial 'powers' like the United States and Germany. By 1900 the USA had overtaken Britain as the manufacturing capital of the world and American exports threatened to damage British trade. The

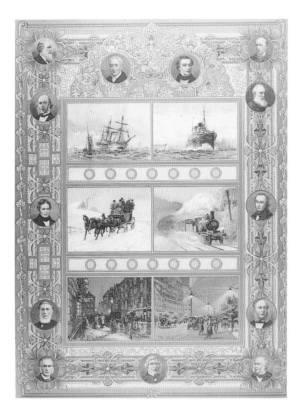

Germans wanted to establish their own overseas empire. By 1900 their navy rivalled the Royal Navy. There were also challenges to British rule from within the Empire. In 1900 Britons found themselves at war in South Africa against the Boers.

One of the major issues facing the politicians of both parties was what to do about poverty. Despite its riches Britain seemed unable or unwilling to cure this ever present and growing problem. A report published in 1902 showed that nearly a third of the population lived in poverty. Those in work often suffered from low wages, poor and dangerous working conditions and slum housing. Those without work, the desperately poor, suffered from malnutrition, sickness and poor health. There were no pensions for the old and many of them ended their lives in the workhouses.

By 1900 there were growing demands for change. Many working-class people still believed that this could be achieved by the Liberal Party which they supported in large numbers. In some industrial towns and cities people had begun to put their hope in a new party – the Independent Labour Party. Wales was in the forefront of this political challenge. In 1900 the Welsh voters of Merthyr Tydfil elected a Scotsman, Keir Hardie, to represent them in Parliament; he was the first Labour MP to be elected in Wales.

The dawn of the twentieth century was a time when new technology was creating changes. These did not affect the lives of many people immediately, but, in the century to come, they would transform the world. They included the motor car and the aeroplane and would soon revolutionise travel. People were coming into contact with new ideas and new fashions. Greater educational opportunities enabled them to read the new popular newspapers such as the *Daily Mail* and *Daily Mirror*. Even the world of entertainment was changing with the advent of cinema. Silent moving pictures had been delighting their audiences for over five years by 1900.

PRE-WAR POLITICS

Liberals and Conservatives: Edwardian Politics and the Election of 1906

Radicalism and Conservatism

By the beginning of the twentieth century British politics was dominated by two parties: the Liberals and the Conservatives. The Liberals were associated with **radicalism**. They sought social, religious and political reform. The Conservatives, or 'Tories', were associated with conservatism. They were against wholesale social or political reform. Many MPs in both parties saw the national interest as one which allowed the upper and middle classes to prosper. They could see the problems of poverty and disease but did not have many ideas about solving them.

SOCIAL CLASS AND THE PARTY SYSTEM

At first neither party truly represented the cause of the poor and the ordinary industrial or agricultural working man or woman. However, this began to change with the passing of the Parliamentary Reform Acts of 1832, 1867 and 1884 when significant numbers of working men were given the power to vote. In fact, after 1884 almost half of Britain's voters were working class. It was during this time of political change that the demand for social reform grew. By 1900, most working-class voters came to see the Liberals as the party to represent their views.

The Conservatives in Government

The Conservatives could count on being the 'natural choice' of the middle and upper classes. This ensured a succession of election victories. Between 1885 and 1905 the Conservatives governed the country for 17 years. The Conservative prime ministers, Salisbury (1886–1902) and Balfour (1902–05), devoted a great deal of their time to foreign affairs and they tended to neglect Britain's problems at home. They were reluctant to tackle poverty because of the high costs involved. They wished to avoid introducing reforms to improve wages and working conditions because they did not want to upset their traditional supporters, the industrialists and landowners.

In 1895 Salisbury chose to ignore a report of the Royal Commission on Labour which showed that the average worker needed at least 25s. (£1.25) a week to live on. In fact, nearly half the British workforce earned little more than 14s. (70p). There were some successes with the Workmen's Compensation Act of 1897, which allowed injured workers to claim compensation from their employers, and Balfour's Education Act of 1902

No. 155.

PROTECTION
v.
FREE TRADE.

Striking Comparisons.

The reports on the cost of living in British, German and French towns published by our Board of Trade give the following general conclusions:—

WAGES PER HOUR.
Where a Briton earns 5s. in wages,
A German earns 3s. 9d.,
A Frenchman earns 3s. 2½d.

HOURS OF LABOUR.
Where a Briton works 100 hours,
A German works 111 hours,
A Frenchman works 117 hours.

HOUSE RENTS.
Where a Briton pays 5s. in rent,
A German pays 6s. 1d. for similar accommodation,
A Frenchman pays 4s. 10d.; but
"his housing accommodation is as a rule decidedly inferior in quality."

WEEKLY BUDGETS.
Where a Briton spends 5s. on food and fuel,
A German spends 5s. 10d. on the same quantity,
A Frenchman spends 5s. 10d.
WHICH IS BEST OFF, THE FREE TRADE BRITON OR THE PROTECTED FRENCHMAN OR GERMAN?

SOURCE A

An election leaflet from 1903.

SOURCE B

'A Free Trade Forecast' – a party political poster from 1906.

SOURCE C

'Flattening Him Out' – another political poster from 1906.

which established 140 Local Education Authorities (LEAs) to run and fund local schools more effectively. However, it was too little too late, and by the election of 1906 the tide had turned against the Conservatives.

The Election of 1906

The 1906 election saw a massive Liberal victory by 377 seats to the Conservatives' 157. In Wales the victory was even more impressive; 33 out of 34 of the MPs elected were Liberals and no Conservative MPs represented Wales. As a result of their majority the new Liberal government under Campbell-Bannerman was able to push through the social reforms it had long promised the voters. It also promised to concentrate on domestic rather than foreign issues and to work with the trade unions rather than oppose them. The Conservatives, meanwhile, were deeply unpopular because they had promised no such reforms. They had attacked the power of the unions and, to make matters worse, they disagreed among themselves, over the major issue of **tariff reform**. The Liberals and a number of Conservatives, including Balfour, believed in free trade, but other Conservatives argued that **protectionism** was the only way British trade could compete with foreign imported goods. The Conservatives managed to survive their problems and within five years they had recovered their political strength. However, for the next decade the Liberals governed the country.

A contemporary print showing the victorious Liberal MPs taking their seats in the House of Commons after the 1906 election.

1 a) List the differences between the Conservative and Liberal Parties.
   b) Why did support steadily:
   (i) increase for the Liberals and
   (ii) decrease for the Conservatives in the period before 1906?

2 a) Study the sources carefully. What message(s) is each source trying to convey to the voters?
   b) Which of the political parties was responsible for producing each of the sources?
   c) In your view, which of the sources would have the greater impact on the voters?

PRE-WAR POLITICS

Poverty and the Poor: Edwardian Society in Crisis?

Towards the end of the nineteenth century the issues of public health and poverty were attracting a great deal of critical comment.

SOURCE A

Annual Report of the Charity Organisation Society (1876). This charity was set up by a group of wealthy philanthropists who believed the poor could best be helped by giving them the means to help themselves.

> The poor should meet the ordinary problems of life, relying not on charity but on their own thrift and self-help. The worker knows that:
> 1. temporary sickness will sometimes visit his household;
> 2. times of slackness of work will occasionally come;
> 3. if he has a large family he is incapable of work.
> All these are the ordinary problems of life. If the worker thinks they will be met by State aid he will make no effort to meet them himself.

Booth and Rowntree

One of the pioneers of social reform was Charles Booth, a wealthy and successful Liverpool shipping merchant who spent over 15 years gathering information on the lives of working people in London. His intention had been to show that people were not as poor as some early social reformers had argued. Faced with the horrible reality of what he found, Booth was forced to change his views and between 1892 and 1903 he published the results of his work in *The Life and Labour of the People of London*.

Seebohm Rowntree, a rich cocoa industrialist from the north, carried out a similar survey based on a house-to-house study in his home city of York. His research showed that an average working-class family of two adults and three children needed a minimum weekly income of one pound to survive. However, Rowntree's published survey of 1901 revealed that nearly 28 per cent of the population of the city lived below this minimum. According to Rowntree's calculations there were two kinds of poverty: primary and secondary. Those suffering primary poverty were mainly without work and could not even afford to buy food. Secondary poverty affected mainly those in low paid or casual employment who earned enough to buy food and possibly to pay the rent but who could not afford items like clothes or shoes.

SOURCE B

An extract from Mrs Pember Reeves' study of working-class life in London, *Round about a Pound a Week* (1913).

> How does a man bring up a family on 20s. [£1.00] a week? 4s. [20p] a week is allowed for food for a child boarded out by the poor law. Assume a family of 4 children. For a woman with 4 children, 4s. [20p] for food for each child is ridiculous. Even at half of that, food for the children would cost 8s. [40p]: if we allow the same for the parents, the 6 people spend 12s. [60p] on food. That leaves 8s.; rent may come to 6 [30p] or 7s. [35p]. How can the woman manage on 1 [5p] or 2s. [10p] a week for coal, gas, insurance, clothes or cleaning materials?

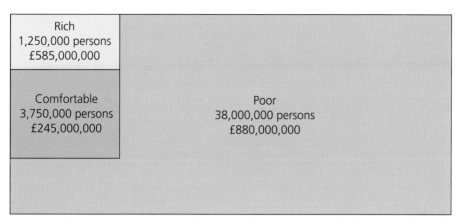

SOURCE C

Adapted from the reformer Chiozza Money's book *Riches and Poverty* (1905).

Wales

The situation in Wales was as bad if not worse than in England. In 1893 Rhondda's chief medical officer reported on the pollution found in the river which 'contains a large proportion of human excrement, offal and entrails from the slaughterhouse, the rotten carcasses of animals, cats and dogs and street refuse'. A 1911 survey showed a death rate of 380 children per 1,000 born in South Wales. Another problem was overcrowding. An 1851 Census return for Merthyr Tydfil revealed a family of seven and their five lodgers living in a two-bedroom house. Local and national governments were slow to act – between 1890 and 1909 only 776 houses were built in Wales.

Changing Attitudes

The belief that poverty was a crime or a sign of bad character which was the fault of the poor began to change towards compassion and sympathy. Social reformers had long been complaining about the problems of poverty but their warnings had been ignored by both Liberal and Conservative governments. This caused some to form social societies with the aim of promoting social reform and in time they came to be called socialists and their ideas **socialism**. However, Booth and Rowntree contributed to a more general change in attitude to the relief of the poor. The Liberal leader Campbell-Bannerman was shocked by the reports and he used Rowntree's figures for York to estimate that nearly 33 per cent of the British nation were living, as he put it, 'on the verge of hunger'.

The Conservatives and Liberals disagreed on how best to help the poor.

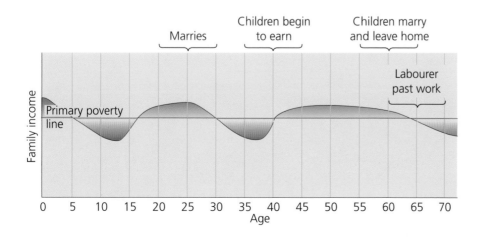

SOURCE D

'The Cycle of Poverty', from S. Rowntree's report, *Poverty: A Study of Town Life* (1901).

SOURCE E

A photograph of two anonymous and homeless paupers (c. 1902).

SOURCE F

An extract from C. Booth, *The Life and Labour of the People of London* (1892–1903).

... brought up in stifling [airless] rooms, with scanty food, in the midst of births and deaths, year after year ... Their life is the life of savages ... their food is of the [poorest quality] and their only luxury is drink ... From these come the battered figures who slouch through the streets ... These are the worst class of corner men who hang round the doors of public houses... They give no useful service, they create no wealth, more often they destroy it ... those who are able to wash the mud away may find some gems in it.

Many Conservatives and some Liberals believed that there was need only for a limited reform, such as improving the workhouses. Other Liberals and an increasing number of socialists wanted to get rid of them. They wanted to establish a system of benefits for the poor which would be paid for by higher taxes. But the Conservatives opposed any increase in taxation.

SOURCE G

A contemporary photograph of miners' houses in Senghennydd (1913).

Mr Charles Booth's paper on State pensions for the aged poor ... proves that pauperism is most probably not, as we have all been taught, due to drunkenness, vice and laziness but to ... sickness and old age. These, according to Mr Booth's unimpeachable [reliable] figures, are the chief cause of poverty.

SOURCE H

An extract from *The Observer*, 20 December 1891.

We have found respectable old women annoyed by the presence of noisy and dirty idiots. We have ourselves seen ... pregnant women forced to work side by side with women so physically deformed ... We have more than once seen young children in bed with minor illnesses next to women of bad character under treatment for infectious disease, whilst other women in the same ward were dying of cancer and senile decay.

SOURCE I

Adapted from a report by a Royal Commission on workhouses (1909).

SOURCE J

A photograph of women at meal time in a St Pancras workhouse (c. 1901).

1. **Sources B, C, D and E are different types of historical evidence. What contribution does each make to the study of poverty in the Edwardian period?**

2. **What, according to Charles Booth (source F) and *The Observer* (source H), were the chief causes of poverty in late Victorian and Edwardian Britain?**

3. **Compare sources A and B. How far had attitudes changed towards the poor between 1876 and 1913?**

4. **Which source or sources might an historian wishing to write a book on poverty in Edwardian Britain find most useful? Explain your choice.**

'New' Liberalism and the Liberal Social Reforms, 1906–14

The Liberal Party that won the general election of 1906 under Campbell-Bannerman had new ideas. Younger party radicals like David Lloyd George and Winston Churchill believed that the poor and needy urgently required help from the state. Lloyd George and Churchill agreed with Rowntree's view that the real problem of poverty in Britain was due to one or more of the following: unemployment or low wages, death or injury of the main wage earner, old age, sickness, large families and little or no education. Herbert Asquith became leader of the Liberals and Prime Minister in 1908. He wanted the Liberals to be seen as the party of reform so he supported and encouraged Lloyd George's radical ideas.

Liberal Reforms: Campbell-Bannerman 1906–8

SOURCE A

This cartoon appeared in *Punch* before the passing of the Old Age Pensions Act in 1908. Lloyd George is shown to be robbing the rich (through higher taxes) in order to cover the cost of pensions.

THE PHILANTHROPIC HIGHWAYMAN.

Mr. Lloyd-George. "*I'LL* MAKE 'EM PITY THE AGED POOR!"

SOURCE B

'The New Year's Gift'. This *Punch* cartoon appeared in 1909, after the passing of the Old Age Pension Act, as the first payments are claimed.

The Campbell-Bannerman government believed that the educational and social needs of children should be met first. In 1906 Parliament passed the Education (Provision of Meals) Act which provided local authorities with funds to provide a school meals service for the very poor. The government realised that for many poor children this would be their only hot meal of the day. In spite of attacks by both Conservatives and 'Old' Liberals who thought this Act interfered with parenting responsibility, it succeeded. By 1914 over 150,000 children were eating school meals daily. In 1907 the Education (Grammar Schools) Act gave many working-class children the opportunity to attend secondary schools without having to pay the fees. In the same year the government set up the Schools Medical Inspection Service which ordered local authorities to have all pupils in their schools inspected at least once a year by trained doctors and nurses.

The Liberal government turned next to the problems of the old and in 1908 Parliament passed an Old Age Pensions Act. The Act enabled people over the age of 70 with an income of less than £21 per year to claim a pension. This amounted to 5s. (25p) per person every week or £13 per year. Although the pension, which was **means-tested**, was not that generous it did remove the immediate threat of the workhouse or charity for the old.

When the Old Age Pensions began, life was transformed for [the] aged... They were relieved of anxiety. They were suddenly rich. Independent for life. At first when they went to the Post Office to draw it, tears of gratitude would run down the cheeks of some, and they would say, as they picked up their money, 'God Bless that Lord George' (for they could not believe that one so powerful and generous could be a plain 'Mr') and 'God Bless you, miss', and there were flowers from their garden ... for the girl who merely handed them the money.

SOURCE C

An extract from Flora Thompson's autobiographical novel, *Lark Rise to Candleford* (1939).

Nearly 400,000 old people claimed the first payments in 1909 at a cost to the government of £1.2 million. This was an important step towards the setting up of a **welfare state** where taxes were used to pay for the relief of the poor and aged.

In 1906 Asquith, the Chancellor of the Exchequer, introduced an improved Workmen's Compensation Act which forced employers to compensate all workers earning less than £200 per year if they suffered injury at work. In the same year the Trades Disputes Act was passed which gave back to the unions the legal power to strike.

Liberal Reforms: Asquith 1908–14

Asquith was determined to pass laws to help the working classes, particularly those on low incomes with little security. When he became Prime Minister he appointed Lloyd George as Chancellor of the Exchequer and Churchill as President of the Board of Trade. In 1909 Churchill ensured the passing of the Trade Boards Act which established teams of government inspectors to check on the working conditions and pay of those employed in the so-called 'sweated industries' like box-making, sack-making and 'slop work' or cheap garment-making.

Influenced by William Beveridge's research for his book *Unemployment*, Lloyd George wanted to help the poor and unemployed find work. In 1909 Parliament passed the Labour Exchange Act which set up a chain of labour exchanges throughout the country where employers could advertise their needs and where those seeking work could get the necessary information. Eighty-three exchanges were set up in 1910. Unfortunately, Lloyd George's attempt to raise the funds for all of this in his Budget of 1909 caused a political crisis (see pages 18–21). The Conservatives were determined to oppose him and even some Liberals were unhappy with the proposals. In the face of stiff opposition, Lloyd George, with Asquith's support, persisted with the reform programme.

Towards a Welfare State?

Lloyd George had for some time been planning to introduce a radical social reform which would lay the foundations of a welfare state. In 1911 he steered through Parliament the National Health Insurance Act. Known as the National Insurance part 1, the Act set up a scheme whereby all manual workers earning less than £3 per week or £160 per year would be entitled to receive free medical attention and a payment of 10s. (50p) per week for 26 weeks if absent from work due to illness, after which a disability pension of 5s. (25p) paid weekly would be available. To pay for the scheme an insured workman would contribute 4d. (just under 2p) a week, his employer 3d. (just over 1p) and the government 2d. (just under 1p) Since the scheme's success depended on the regular contributions of the workers and employers, Lloyd George made it compulsory.

The scheme was limited to certain trades and occupations and it did not cover families but only insured workmen. This meant that working husbands would have to continue paying for medical treatment of wives and children.

The National Insurance Act part 2 (1913) dealt with unemployment insurance. Its provisions are described in source D.

SOURCE D

An extract from William Beveridge, *Unemployment* (1912).

The insured trades were building, shipbuilding, mechanical engineering, ironfounding, construction of vehicles and sawmilling. Every workman in those trades had to have an 'unemployment book'. To this book the employer had for each week of employment to fix a 5d. insurance stamp, and was entitled to deduct half the value from the workman's wages.

[If a workman became unemployed, he claimed] 7s. a week up to a maximum of 15 weeks at an Employment Exchange. He proved his unemployment and his capacity [ability] to work by signing an unemployment register there daily.

SOURCE E

A poster issued by the Liberal Party to publicise Lloyd George's National Insurance Scheme (1911).

	In receipt of relief in the workhouse	Outdoor relief	Total in receipt of relief
7 October, 1908	78,114	45,830	123,944
7 October, 1909	78,260	43,810	122,070
7 October, 1910	77,503	40,679	118,182
7 October, 1911	75,233	29,634	104,867

SOURCE F

Official figures for London, quoted in *The Times* (October 1911).

1 (a) What message about Lloyd George's old age pensions scheme is *Punch* trying to convey in source A and source B?
(b) Why is Lloyd George drawn tending a sick man rather than a sick woman in source E?

2 (a) List the Liberal reforms and under each one briefly explain who they were designed to help and how they were intended to work.
(b) Why might some contemporaries have:
(i) welcomed and **(ii)** opposed the Liberal social reforms?

PRE-WAR POLITICS

Democracy in Crisis? The 'People's Budget' of 1909

Lords and Commons

Before the nineteenth century the House of Lords was more powerful than the House of Commons. The House of Lords consisted of Peers of the Realm (titled nobility) such as barons, earls and dukes together with the bishops of the Church of England. They were not elected, but took their seats by right of birth or in the case of the Church by right of office. In contrast, the MPs who took their seats in the House of Commons did so by right of election. Their membership of Parliament was not for life but until the next general election. Compared with today, there was little real democracy since many MPs were elected by small numbers of influential landowners and businessmen. Indeed, until the first half of the nineteenth century, there was little to choose between a member of the Lords or Commons, because the representatives of both Houses were generally wealthy landowners with similar social and political views and were often related to each other.

In the nineteenth century there were many in the Commons who resisted change. But the pressure for reform from inside and outside Parliament led to the Parliamentary Reform Acts. Other reforms followed such as the Ballot Act of 1872, which set up the secret system of voting. The Redistribution Act of 1885 redrew **constituency** boundaries which gave places like Manchester and Merthyr Tydfil more representation thus making voting fairer. As a result of these reforms the balance of power gradually shifted away from the Lords to the Commons. Britain was becoming a democracy.

Crisis over the Budget

In the Budget of 1909 the Chancellor, Lloyd George, stated that some £16 million extra in taxes would be needed to help the poor. He proposed that income tax for those with an annual income of more than £3,000 should be raised from the rate of five per cent to eight per cent. In addition, death duties (a tax on property left by rich landowners) would be raised to 15 per cent. A further tax on the profits of land sales would also be imposed. This was one of the most radical budgets ever proposed.

The Liberal majority in the Commons meant that the Conservatives could not prevent the Budget from being passed. However, for the Budget's proposals to become law it needed to be passed in the House of Lords, where the majority of its members were Conservative supporters. The Lords refused to pass the Budget. Lloyd George responded by persuading Asquith to call a general election to prove that the voters supported the Budget. The Liberals won and the Lords passed the Budget. Victory in the election had shown the House of Lords who really governed Britain.

RICH FARE.

The Giant Lloyd-Gorgibuster : " Fee, fi, fo, fat,
I smell the blood of a Plutocrat ;
Be he alive or be he dead,
I'll grind his bones to make my bread."

[April 28, 1909.]

SOURCE A

A cartoon in *Punch* expressing the opinion of some of its readers towards the Budget (1909). (A plutocrat is someone in power because of their wealth.)

The Parliament Act of 1911

Lloyd George decided to increase pressure on the Lords by drawing up an Act which would reduce their power to stop Bills being passed into law once the Commons had accepted them. The Lords fought back and refused to pass Lloyd George's Parliament Bill. He accused them of ignoring the wishes of the people. So Asquith again called an election to prove the point. The Liberals were victorious once more but this time the Lords still refused to pass the Bill. Lloyd George said that the very principle of democracy was at stake.

To solve the crisis Asquith asked the King, George V, for his support. The King agreed that if the Lords continued to reject the Bill he would create over 100 new peers – all of them Liberal. The threat worked and the Bill was passed. The Upper House could never again interfere with the democratic process; the most they could do was delay the passing of new laws for two years. To compensate for the increase in power of the Commons it was agreed that elections would now be held every five rather than every seven years.

> The Budget is introduced ... for the provision for the Aged and Deserving Poor. It is time it were done. It is a shame for a rich country like ours ... that it should allow those who have toiled all their days to end in penury [poverty] and possible starvation...

SOURCE B

(above) An extract from a famous speech delivered by Lloyd George in Limehouse (1909).

> The proposed taxes ... appear to be without parallel in our history... The motive which inspires [them] is not the national welfare but... a desire to strike at the rich.

SOURCE C

(above) An extract from a speech delivered by the Duke of Marlborough debating the Budget in the House of Lords (1909).

> A fully equipped duke costs as much to keep as two 'dreadnoughts' [British battleship], and dukes are just as great a terror, and they last longer.
>
> They have no qualifications ... they need not be sound in either body or mind. They only require a certificate of birth – just to prove that they are the first of the litter. You would not choose a spaniel on these principles.

SOURCE D

(above) Extracts from a speech delivered by Lloyd George to an audience in Wolverhampton (1909).

SOURCE E

(right) A photograph of the Houses of Parliament (c. 1910).

SOURCE F

The response of one newspaper to the House of Lords' rejection of the 'People's Budget'.

1 a) What did Lloyd George mean by his reference to the 'Deserving Poor' in source B?
b) Why did the Duke of Marlborough (source C) think that Lloyd George's attack on the Lords was motivated by spite and envy?

2 When Lloyd George heard that the Lords had rejected his Budget he said 'Let them realise what they are doing. They are forcing a revolution and they will get it …' What do you think he meant by this?

3 At the age of 81, a year before he died, Lloyd George accepted a peerage from the King and he became the Earl Lloyd George of Dwyfor with a seat in the House of Lords. In view of his earlier attitude to the Lords:
a) Why were so many people shocked and outraged by this?
b) Why do you think he accepted the peerage?
c) What might it tell us about Lloyd George?

The Rise of Labour

The Parliamentary Reform Acts of the nineteenth century gradually gave working-class men the opportunity to voice their concerns about issues which directly affected them such as poverty, unemployment, ill-health and poor housing. This brought about a change in the attitude of the Liberals and Conservatives towards the working classes since they realised that their votes would be crucial in winning future elections. The radicals within the Liberal Party were particularly keen to win the working-class vote. In some strongly working-class areas, the Liberals agreed to support the election of working men to Parliament. These working-class MPs came to be called **Lib-Labs** and by 1906 their number had risen to 24.

The Independent Labour Party

However, some social reformers were growing impatient with the Liberals. They believed that the only way for the poor to help themselves was by electing their own independent representatives to Parliament. Many of the working classes felt that the Lib-Labs did not represent their views so they decided to form their own party. This proved difficult since they had neither the money nor the support of powerful trade unions. Yet despite these problems they began to organise themselves into local socialist societies. By 1893 these societies had come together to form the Independent Labour Party (ILP), founded and led by Keir Hardie (see his *Profile* on page 26).

Labour MPs pictured in the House of Commons (1910).

Keir Hardie realised that the new party was too weak to have much effect in Parliament so he aimed to strengthen its position in local government. Between 1895 and 1916 the number of Labour councillors increased significantly. Hardie hoped that Labour's growing power in Britain's towns and cities would put pressure on the older political parties to act in the cause of social reform.

THE TRADE UNIONS AND THE LRC

Hardie knew that the ILP needed the support and financial backing of the trade unions if it was ever to succeed in becoming a strong political party. His plea for support led to the formation of the Labour Representation Committee (LRC) in 1900. The LRC was given the task of recruiting trade union members to the Labour movement and setting up a parliamentary party strong enough to take on the Liberals and Conservatives. At first Hardie and the Labour Party met with some resistance. Many unions were reluctant to finance a party which seemed incapable of representing them in Parliament. Others wished to continue their support for the Liberals. It was many years before the trade unions changed their attitude towards the Labour Party.

The Labour Movement in Wales

Although the valleys of south-east Wales and Merthyr in particular were heavily industrialised, the Labour movement had found little support. There were no Welsh delegates at the Bradford Labour conference which led to the setting up of the ILP in 1893. For much of the nineteenth century Wales was solidly Liberal and between 1890 and 1914 Welsh Liberal MPs were so numerous and some so talented that they could influence government policy. The average Welsh voter seemed reluctant to support a party (Labour) and an idea (socialism) that appeared foreign and English. By 1906 only four branches of the ILP had been established in Wales – at Cardiff, Treharris, Merthyr Tydfil and Wrexham.

However, attitudes in Wales began to change. Before 1906 few working Welshmen were members of unions. Out of a workforce of 250,000 miners, for example, less than 45,000 were organised in trade unions. But

SOURCE A

Bryn O' Callaghan, *A History of the Twentieth Century* (1987).

Not all union members ... supported the Labour Party. One union member who backed the Liberals was W.V. Osborne. Osborne took his union to court to stop it handing over money from members' subscriptions to the Labour Party. He won his case. In the Osborne Judgement in 1909 the judges forbade the unions to give money to political parties.

The Osborne Judgement meant that the Labour Party would be starved of funds to pay its MPs and its election bills. The Liberal government solved the problem, in return for Labour backing it in a quarrel with the Conservatives ... in 1911 Parliament voted all MPs a salary of £400 a year. Then, in 1913, the Trade Union Act said that unions could give money to political parties.

after 1906 this number rose substantially. Hardie and the ILP persuaded more working-class Welshmen that the only way to achieve decent wages and better working conditions was to support a party of workers to represent them in Parliament. In 1900 Hardie was elected the first Labour MP in Wales for Merthyr Tydfil. He held the seat until his death in 1915.

Labour and the 1906 Election

The election proved to be a turning point – not just for the Liberals who won decisively but for Labour also. The day before the election the party changed its name from the ILP to the Labour Party and although they won only 29 of the 670 seats contested in Britain they could no longer be ignored. In 1908 the Party's representation in Parliament nearly doubled when the 24 Lib-Lab MPs finally joined the Labour Party.

During the following eight years the Labour Party tended to support the Liberals and Lloyd George's social and political reforms. This led to some of its members outside Parliament criticising it for not having a socialist programme of its own. Others were disappointed because they thought

SOURCE B

A cartoon from *Punch* showing the uneasy relationship between Labour and the Liberals (1906).

A BIT OF A BREEZE.

C.-B. (*Organ Grinder, to* Independent Labour Party). "AIN'T YOU A-GOIN' TO JOIN IN WITH YOUR FRIEND, MISS?" I. L. P. "NOT ME! SHE AIN'T MY CLASS!"

that the Labour MPs should be opposing the Liberals in Parliament. It was only in local government that Labour was free to govern according to its socialist ideas and principles. Some Labour councils proved to be both popular and successful. Despite these teething problems the party survived and with the financial backing of the unions from 1913 onwards, it grew in strength.

Election date	Parliamentary seats gained in Wales
1880	29 out of 33
1885	30 out of 34
1886	25 out of 36
1892	31 out of 34
1895	25 out of 34
1900	28 out of 34
1906	33 out of 34

SOURCE C

Liberal general election results in Wales (1880–1906).

Election date	Liberals	Labour	Conservative
1906	377	29	157
1918	162	59	338
1922	117	142	347
1923	158	191	258
1924	40	151	419

SOURCE D

Labour, Liberal and Conservative general election results (1906–1924).

SOURCE E

The year 1908 was the turning point in the development of the Labour Party in Wales and, though it was not until 1922 that Labour became the majority party in Wales, it was clearly [growing stronger] from that time. We all recognised that the major task of the Labour Party in Wales was to win the workers from their Liberal allegiance, and it was the 1914–18 War which was finally to achieve this aim. The 1914–18 War began to break up the alliance between the Chapels and the Liberals, and the [quarrel] between Lloyd George and Asquith played a [major] part in this.

An extract from a lecture delivered in 1973 by James Griffiths (1890–1975). He was a Labour MP and first Secretary of State for Wales.

1 a) **What do you learn about the relationship between Labour and the Liberals from sources A and B?**
b) **How might sources A and B contradict each other?**
c) **Why were the consequences of the Osborne Judgement more important than the Judgement itself? Explain your answer.**

2 a) **How useful are the statistics in sources C and D in explaining the strength of the Liberal Party between 1880 and 1924?**
b) **What do you learn about the changes in British party politics from the statistics in source D?**

profile

Keir Hardie

Early Life

James Keir Hardie was born in Lanarkshire in Scotland in 1856, the son of a drunken and unemployed ship's carpenter. As a result of their extreme poverty his younger brother and mother suffered from the effects of chronic ill-health. Since his father was often away from home seeking work, Hardie left school at the age of seven to earn money for the family. He was employed in a Glasgow bakery which expected him to work for twelve and a half hours per day. At the age of 11 he left to work in the mines. Here Hardie prospered. He worked hard to better himself and he spent time getting properly educated. In 1879 at the age of 23 he was elected by his fellow miners to represent them as their union agent. Seven years later he became the first secretary to the Scottish Miners' Federation.

The Politician

Hardie's political ambitions received a blow in 1888 when he tried and failed to gain the support of the Lanarkshire Liberal Association to stand as a Lib-Lab candidate for Parliament. He then stood unsuccessfully as an independent Labour candidate. Despite this setback he set up the Scottish Labour Party, a move which influenced other socialists to do the same across the country. In 1892 he was elected MP for the London constituency of West Ham, a poor and run down part of the city. He informed the electorate that 'Politics is but a football game between the rich Tories and

Keir Hardie's election poster 1888.

VOTE FOR

Home Rule.

Democratic Government.

Justice to Labour

No Monopoly.

No Landlordism

Temperance Reform.

Healthy Homes.

Fair Rents.

Eight-Hour Day.

Work for the Unemployed.

KEIR HARDIE.

Printed and Published by F. W. Scr se & Co. [L.S.C.], 151, Barking Road, Canning Town, London, E.

the rich Liberals and you working men are the ball which they kick vigorously and with grim delight between their goalposts'. Based on his electoral success, Hardie founded the Independent Labour Party (ILP) in 1893.

At first this new party consisted of a small group of socialists, drawn mainly from a few intellectuals and younger working-class people. Neither the unions nor the other political parties took Hardie and his socialists seriously. But Hardie's party continued to recruit members and although most still came from the worse-off workers and the poorer unions he managed to attract some well-educated men like Philip Snowden and Ramsey MacDonald. Like Hardie, they too had been born into poverty and hardship. They brought a certain culture and education to the party and their growing expertise in matters of finance and economics earned the respect of opposition MPs.

Hardie, Labour and Wales

Hardie turned to Wales for support and he found it in Merthyr Tydfil. In the election of 1900 he was elected MP for Merthyr Tydfil by a small majority mainly because of his plans for social reform. However, many thought him a traitor because of his **pacifist** and anti-Boer War views. His Liberal opponent Pritchard Morgan put up posters in Merthyr with the slogan 'Vote for D.A. Thomas and Keir Hardie, both pro-Boers'.

Hardie considered the Welsh to be 'natural socialists' and he worked hard to promote the growth of the party in the country. By 1905, 25 local Labour Associations had been established across Wales, mainly in the industrial valleys of the south east from Aberdare to Blaenavon and from Merthyr south to Cardiff. Soon socialist newspapers were being printed and sold.

Keir Hardie represented Merthyr in Parliament for 15 years. He was liked and respected but his outspoken pacifist views turned even some of his own supporters against him. At the outbreak of the Great War in 1914 he and other leading figures in the Labour Party openly declared their opposition to the fighting. The mood of the people of Merthyr had changed since the days of the Boer War. His attempts to explain his objections to the war resulted in him being threatened at one public meeting in Aberdare. In 1915 he died a broken and humiliated man but his hard work had firmly established the Labour movement in Wales and Britain.

TRECH GWLAD NAC ARGLWYDD

SOURCE B

Keir Hardie's election poster 1906.

1 How might the experiences of Keir Hardie's early life have contributed to his founding of the Labour Party in 1893?

2 a) Explain each of the points raised by Keir Hardie on his election poster of 1888.
b) In your view which of the points would have been: (i) most effective and (ii) least effective in winning him votes?

c) Compare sources A and B. Which in your view is the most effective election campaign poster? Explain your answer.

3 An historian once said 'Were it not for the hard work and leadership of Keir Hardie the Labour Party would never have existed'. Do you agree or disagree with this statement? Explain your answer fully. (For further reading on the Labour Party see pages 22–25.)

'A woman's place ...?' The Suffragette Movement

In 1906 the Suffragette Movement had been in existence for 40 years but there was little to celebrate. It had failed to achieve its primary aim of 'votes for women'. However, it had become a mass movement attracting publicity to the cause of women's emancipation. By 1906 the issue of women's suffrage could no longer be ignored.

Early Years

The women's movement began in the mid-1860s as a collection of small, local and quite separate pressure groups. Some of these early women's suffrage societies were set up in the industrial towns and cities of the north of England like Manchester and Sheffield where they demanded equal rights with men. The members of these societies were mainly from the middle and upper classes and their first success was in gaining the right to work.

Careers in teaching, nursing and the civil service became available because of better education. However, the majority of women from the lower classes received little or no education. They had no choice but to work in domestic service or in the so-called 'sweated industries' such as the cotton factories or home dressmaking.

EARLY ORGANISATIONS

In 1897 a leading **Suffragette**, Millicent Fawcett, realised that unless the various societies joined together to form one united organisation then the cause of women's suffrage was likely to be lost. The result was the National Union of Women's Suffrage Societies (NUWSS) which campaigned against those opposed to women's suffrage by publishing pamphlets like the one shown on the left.

Many men and some women, including Queen Victoria, believed that women were not clever enough to understand politics. A majority of MPs in Parliament tended to support this prejudiced view of women. The NUWSS hoped to persuade these politicians to grant them the franchise (the right to vote). It believed that the political party most likely to be sympathetic to their cause would be the Liberals. But, despite promises of change, Liberal governments did nothing.

By 1903 younger Suffragettes had lost patience with the Liberal Party so they set up the Women's Social and Political Union (WSPU). Its founder, Mrs Emmeline Pankhurst, gradually came to believe that more drastic action was necessary if they were to be successful. Within a few short years Mrs Pankhurst and her Suffragettes were living up to their motto of 'Deeds not words'.

SOURCE A

A Suffragette pamphlet (c. 1898).

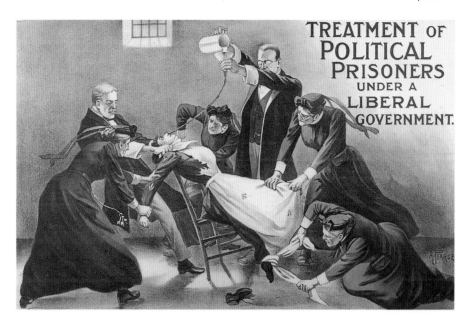

SOURCE B

A Suffragette poster (c. 1910).

Militancy and Violence

The WSPU began a militant campaign which involved interrupting political meetings, organising public marches and window-smashing demonstrations. The Suffragettes attracted even more publicity by chaining themselves to the railings at Buckingham Palace and Downing Street. They also began publishing their exploits in the Suffragette newspaper *Votes for Women* which first appeared in 1907. The government responded by imprisoning the lawbreakers. The Suffragettes hit back by going on hunger-strike.

Marion Dunlop was the first to try this new tactic in 1909 after the government refused to treat her as a political prisoner. Within four days of going on hunger-strike the authorities gave in and released her. Soon other Suffragettes were employing the same tactic. An embarrassed but angry government tried a new approach – force feeding. It was a deeply unpopular policy which caused an outcry from those who did not support the Suffragettes as well as those who did.

... some of the themes that agitated Edwardian England were less powerful in Wales. [Here] the Suffragettes made little headway. More than most parts of Britain, Wales ... believed that a woman's place was in the home and in chapel, certainly not in the polling-booth, even though Lloyd George and many other Welsh Liberals voted for women's suffrage in the House [of Commons].

SOURCE C

Adapted from Kenneth Morgan, *Rebirth of a Nation: Wales 1880–1980* (1981).

1 **Compare sources A and B. In what ways did the Suffragette message change between 1898 and 1910?**

2 **a) Explain what you understand by the Suffragette motto 'Deeds not words'?**

b) How does the motto, adopted in 1903, help to explain the change in the methods used by the Suffragettes to promote their cause in England and Wales?

FOCUS

Emily Davison and the 1913 Derby

By 1910 Herbert Asquith, the leader of the Liberal government came to believe that a women's suffrage Act might be the only way to stop the violence. However, when Asquith announced that a general election was to be held in November 1910 the issue of women's suffrage was dropped. The Liberals were afraid of losing votes if they supported it.

The 'Cat and Mouse Act'

In 1913 the frustrated Suffragettes turned to destroying property. This resulted in even more of them being imprisoned. In an effort to punish hunger-strikers without force feeding them the government passed the so-called 'Cat and Mouse Act'. This meant that prisoners suffering from the effects of hunger would be released, only to be re-arrested later when they were better. The scene was set for bitter conflict.

THE CAT AND MOUSE ACT

PASSED BY THE LIBERAL GOVERNMENT

THE LIBERAL CAT
ELECTORS VOTE AGAINST HIM!
KEEP THE LIBERAL OUT!

BUY AND READ 'THE SUFFRAGETTE' PRICE 1D

SOURCE A

(above) A Suffragette poster attacking the 'Prisoners' Temporary Discharge for Ill-Health Act' or the 'Cat and Mouse Act' (1913).

The Derby of 1913 will be long remembered ... [for] the desperate act of a woman who rushed from the rails on to the course, apparently from some mad notion that she could spoil the race. She did not interfere with the race, but she nearly killed a jockey as well as herself, and she brought down a valuable horse. It was impossible to avoid her. She was ridden down, the horse turned a complete somersault and fell upon its rider.

That the horse was the king's was doubtless an accident, it would need almost miraculous skill or fortune to single out any particular animal ... Whether she intended to commit suicide, or was simply reckless, it is hard to tell ... She is said to be a person well known in the Suffragist Movement, to have a card of a Suffragist association upon her, and to have had the so-called 'Suffragist colours' tied around her waist. It is further alleged that just after she had run out in front of the horse ... a poster bearing the words 'Votes for Women' was raised by a person in the crowd.

A deed of this kind, we need hardly say, is not likely to increase the popularity of any cause with the public. Reckless fanaticism [obsessive behaviour] is not regarded by them as a qualification for the vote. They say that persons who deliberately destroy property and endanger lives must be either desperately wicked or entirely unbalanced.

SOURCE B

(right) Adapted from *The Times*, 5 June 1913.

SOURCE C

A photograph records the incident moments after it happened. The *Daily Sketch*, 9 June 1913.

SOURCE D

Contemporary pictures of Mrs Davison appeared in The *Daily Sketch*, 9 June 1913.

One Suffragette who believed passionately in the cause was Emily Davison. Clutching in her hand a petition, she deliberately threw herself under the hooves of the king's horse. Horse, jockey and woman crashed to the ground. Emily's skull was fractured and she died a little later. The Suffragettes had been provided with a martyr.

SOURCE E

J. Ray, *Britain and the Modern World* (1969).

If she was going to commit suicide... [Emily Davison] would have thrown herself headlong in front of the galloping horse. However, all the evidence on film refutes it. She ran on to the racecourse and she stood sideways on, waiting for the King's horse to come up to her; when it was alongside she thrust out her left hand and tried to grab the reins and of course with the great momentum of a race horse coming towards her at 40 mph she was flung headlong [under its hooves] striking her head and fracturing her skull.

SOURCE F

John Sleight, an historian quoted on BBC Radio 4 (1988).

1 a) What was *The Times'* attitude to the incident? Explain fully.
b) In your opinion is source E more useful than D in helping to understand what Emily Davison was trying to do at the Derby?
c) 'Sources B and C are primary evidence and source E is secondary therefore B and C are more reliable than E.' Do you agree with this statement? Explain your answer.

2 Using the text and sources, was Emily Davison's death the result of an accident or a carefully laid plan to commit suicide?

3 What effect would her death have had on the Suffragette cause?

OVERVIEW

Consider the following key question. To what extent was there a demand and need for social and political reform in the period 1906–14?

UNIT *2*

Wales in Industrial Britain

> **KEY ISSUE:**
> *1906–14: The golden age of Welsh heavy industry?*

Wales as a whole made a massive contribution to the great industrial revolution which began in the mid to late eighteenth century. Indeed, south-east Wales was among the first areas in Britain to experience its unstoppable progress.

Industrialisation

The iron and coal industries were the first to be developed, soon followed by other heavy industries such as slate, tinplate and copper. These industries required a great deal of capital investment if they were to make a profit. With the exception of the coal industry much of the capital came from outside Wales, from rich landowners and businessmen in England. These investors brought with them English and Scottish managers and engineers. However, the bulk of the workforce were native Welshmen. Between 1860 and 1910 over 320,000 people migrated into the coalfields of South Wales from the Welsh countryside. This in turn led to the rapid urbanisation of the South Wales valleys in order to keep pace with the massive growth in population.

TRANSPORT

The industrialisation of Wales and the economic success it enjoyed may never have occurred had there not been a similar revolution in transport and communications. The chief means of transporting industrial goods was by rail and sea. The railway network was rapidly expanded while major new

A picture of Craig Ddu quarrymen returning home to Blaenau Ffestiniog down the incline on the slate trolleys or 'wild cars' (c.1907).

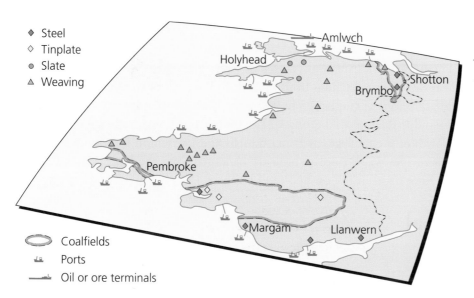

SOURCE A

The major industries of Wales, 1880–1914.

ports were developed at Newport, Cardiff, Swansea, Llanelli and Milford Haven. By 1911 nearly 86,000 people were employed on the railways and at the docks. So rapid and complete had the industrialisation of the country been that an historian, Professor Gareth Jones, has said that 'Wales in the period 1880–1914 was a vibrant, proud, successful country. Industrial wealth had moved Wales from the margins of Britain to a position of world importance'.

Iron and Steel

Steel replaced iron as the main export of Welsh metals from the beginning of the twentieth century. The old iron foundries had been situated far inland at places like Merthyr Tydfil but the new steel plants with the latest technology, such as the Siemens open hearth furnaces, were built on the coast near the great ports of Swansea, Cardiff, Port Talbot and Newport. Steel works were also established in the north east at Brymbo, Deeside and Shotton where the production of sheet-steel was pioneered. In 1902 a sizeable part of Britain's total steel production of 4.85 million tons came from Welsh plants.

Copper, Zinc and Other Metals

The Welsh copper extraction, or copper-smelting industry was based mainly in South Wales, in large industrial plants situated in the areas of Neath and Swansea. It proved to be highly successful and, of the copper smelted in Britain in the last decade of the nineteenth century, 90 per cent came from South Wales. A survey of 1911 revealed that about 3700 were employed in the industry. Although not as large as the copper industry, zinc-smelting was no less important to the economy of South Wales. Based in the region of Swansea, by 1910 the industry was producing nearly 75 per cent of British zinc. The importance of Swansea as a metallurgical centre was recognised by Sir Alfred Mond, a German-Jewish industrialist who came to Britain and in 1902 built the biggest nickel works in the world at Clydach, near Swansea. In 1910 he was elected the Liberal MP for Swansea.

Tinplate

The tinplate industry was centred in west Wales. Just before the First World War 82 works stretching from Llanelli to Port Talbot were producing over 848,000 tons of tinplate, 544,000 tons of which were for export. In 1911 the industry employed around 21,000 men and it was responsible for the growth of such villages as Pontarddulais and Gorseinon into flourishing towns. The Welsh tinplate industry benefited from the huge demand for its tin from firms in the canned-food business.

Coal

Coal was the largest and most rapidly expanding industry in Wales. For example, the production of coal rose from 16 million tons in 1871 to 30 million in 1891, reaching its peak of 56.8 million tons in 1913. The export of coal from Swansea docks rose from 925,000 tons in 1880 to 3.5 million tons in 1913. The South Wales coalfield, which stretched from the Gwendraeth and Amman valleys in the west to the Rhymney and Sirhowy valleys in the east, was particularly large and productive. At the beginning of the Great War South Wales was producing about one third of the world's coal exports and was responsible for the employment of over 250,000 men. The coal industry also grew in north-east Wales and, by 1911, 14,500 men were employed in the coalfields of Denbighshire and Flintshire. (See also Unit 2, *King Coal.*)

SOURCE B

(below) A map of the South Wales coalfield.

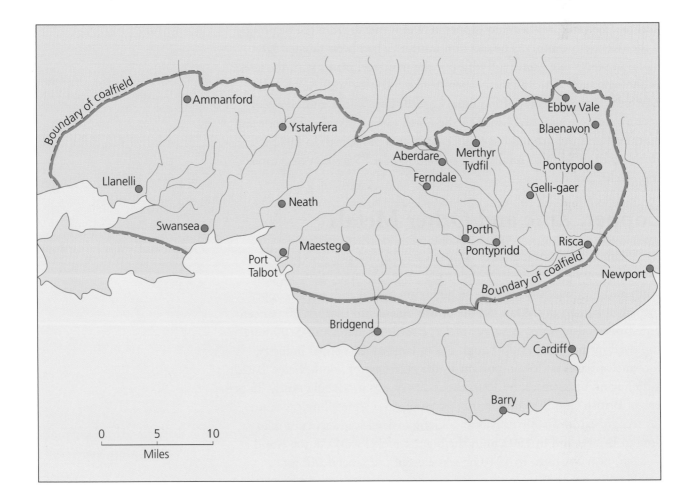

Slate

The slate industry was as important to north-west Wales as coal was to the south. Slate was responsible for the growth and prosperity of quarry towns like Bethesda, Llanberis, Blaenau Ffestiniog and Corris and for ports such as Portmadoc and Port Dinorwic. At its peak in 1898 the industry employed 16,000 men and nearly 70 per cent of British slate was quarried in North Wales. The Penrhyn and Dinorwic quarries were the biggest in the world. Unfortunately, the disastrous Penrhyn strike of 1900–3 led to closure and unemployment. By 1903 the industry was in crisis. A sharp fall in the demand for Welsh slate led to the collapse of the once prosperous overseas market. By 1909 the number of men employed in the slate industry had fallen to 13,000.

SOURCE C

A group of workers at Pantyffynnon colliery near Ammanford pose for the camera (1904).
Pantyffynnon was one of nearly two dozen pits in the Amman Valley alone.

1 What do the terms: (i) capital and (ii) urbanisation mean?

2 How useful are: (i) maps like sources A and B
(ii) photographs like source C in contributing to an understanding of what industrial Wales was like in Edwardian times?

3 'In 1910 Wales was the industrial capital of the world.' Give reasons to support this statement.

King Coal

A photograph of a typical Welsh colliery above ground: Llwynypia Colliery in the Rhondda (c.1910). This pit was owned by D.A. Thomas (see his *Profile* in Unit 2) and it became the scene for one of the worst riots in Welsh mining history.

Coal had been mined in Wales for centuries but it was not until the eighteenth century that its potential as a source of wealth and power was fully realised. The blast furnaces of the iron foundries demanded huge amounts of coal to power them which in turn led to the rapid expansion of the industry. As the nineteenth century progressed the iron industry went into decline to be replaced by steel making; but the coal industry continued to develop. The centre of the coal industry became the Rhondda valley, which in 1913 employed around 41,000 men and produced over 9.5 million tons of coal.

The Coal Barons

Entrepreneurs like David Davies of Llandinam (d. 1890), and W.T. Lewis of Merthyr Tydfil (d. 1914) found new markets for Welsh coal, such as powering the ships of the Royal Navy or as a domestic fuel for London householders. Soon another generation of capitalist coalowners like D.A. Thomas and Thomas Powell began to plan on a larger scale and they set up coal companies such as the Cambrian Combine, Powell Duffryn and Ocean Coal. These companies ran hundreds of pits, employed thousands of

A plan of a typical Welsh colliery below ground: Universal Colliery, Senghennydd (1913). This pit was the scene for one of the worst mining disasters in British mining history. 439 men lost their lives.

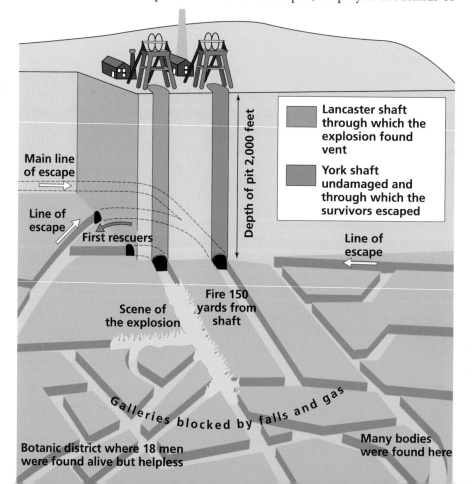

Main line of escape

Line of escape

First rescuers

Depth of pit 2,000 feet

Lancaster shaft through which the explosion found vent

York shaft undamaged and through which the survivors escaped

Line of escape

Fire 150 yards from shaft

Scene of the explosion

Galleries blocked by falls and gas

Botanic district where 18 men were found alive but helpless

Many bodies were found here

men and made their owners and directors wealthy and influential. As a further mark of their success these men were given titles and seats in the House of Lords. Davies was created Baron Davies of Llandinam, Lewis became Baron Merthyr of Senghennydd and the richest of them all, D.A. Thomas was created Baron Rhondda. (See his *Profile* on pages 40 and 41.)

Transport, Railways and Ports

The coalmasters were quick to spot the potential of Welsh coal as a product for export. But for this they needed the means to transport the coal from their mines in the upper reaches of the valleys to the coastal ports. This led to the construction of railways, some of which were built specifically as coal rather than passenger lines. Railway companies were formed to cope with the demand. The two most famous were the Taff Vale and Rhymney Railway Companies.

However, the growth of the coal industry was so rapid that some railway companies and some ports like Cardiff could not cope with the massive output from the mines. The total volume of coal exports from South Wales had more than tripled in less than 25 years. By the turn of the century the massive Bute docks at Cardiff was joined by new purpose-built coal-exporting ports at Barry and Penarth. (See the following chapter.)

SOURCE C

The mansion-house built at Ferndale for Lewis Davies, a coalowner in the Rhondda valley.

The domestic heating of eastern and central Europe, the railways of France, Italy, Brazil and Argentina, above all the oceanic steam-driven carrying fleet of the world, all rested to a great degree on the expanding production and aggressive marketing of Welsh coal.

SOURCE D

K. Morgan, *Rebirth of a Nation, Wales 1880–1980* (1981).

The hewer [cutter] down in the mine away from the sunlight and fresh air, sometimes in a temperature up to 90 deg., every moment of the day inhaling coal dust, head throbbing with the almost inhuman exertion [effort]; the roof perhaps 18 inches low, perhaps 20 feet high... breathing always noxious [unhealthy] smells due to the absence of any kind of sanitation... liable always to wounds and death from falls of roof and sides and over all the sickening dread of the awful explosion; such a man is entitled to our sympathy and our respect – but what he frequently gets – is abuse.

SOURCE E

Noah Ablett recalls his days as a face worker in the mines in his book *What we want and why* (1922). He became a leading member of the South Wales Miners' Federation and a bitter opponent of D.A. Thomas.

1 **What do you understand by the terms: (i) entrepreneur and (ii) capitalist?**

2 **a) According to sources B and E, what were: (i) the difficulties and (ii) the dangers facing coalminers in the South Wales coalfield?**
   b) According to the text, what rewards might a successful coalowner like D.A. Thomas expect?

3 **How and why did coal become the most important industry in Wales?**

ECONOMIC DEVELOPMENTS

The Development of Cardiff

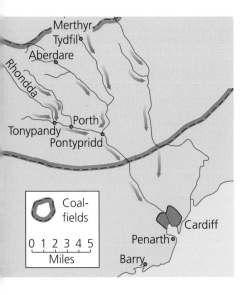

SOURCE A

The South Wales coalfield and the position of Cardiff.

The building of the railways in the mid to late nineteenth century led to the growth and development of ports and towns such as Barry, Penarth, Newport and Cardiff. Although the most spectacular growth occurred at Barry, a town which was almost purpose built to service the coal trade, Cardiff by far outstripped them and all the other towns of Wales. Trade, money, industry and immigration changed the town of Cardiff into the biggest coal exporting port in the world.

The construction of the docks and other sites of industrial importance was followed by massive house building to accommodate the vast numbers of people who migrated to the new metropolis from the small towns of the valleys and rural villages of the vale of Glamorgan and the West of England. Some of these immigrants came from further afield. Italians, Germans, Indians and Somalis all settled to live and work in the international port.

By 1905 Cardiff had become the capital of Wales. A university, sports stadia, and elegant **baroque** buildings, such as the city hall and the national museum, were built within its boundaries. By 1914 the city could also boast a fine park, Cathays, located at its centre. Cardiff was built on the wealth and opportunities brought by coal, which by 1913 dominated the Welsh industrial economy.

SOURCE B

The population growth of Welsh industrial towns, calculated from census returns (1851–1901).

	1851	1901
Merthyr Tydfil	46,378	69,228
Newport	19,323	67,270
Swansea	21,533	94,537
Cardiff	18,351	164,333

SOURCE C

City of Cardiff tourist information leaflet: City Hall (1990).

The Marble Hall has ... in white... Marble, a series of fine statutes entitled 'The Heroes of Wales'. These statutes were installed in 1916 – a year noted more for wholesale death and destruction than for the creation of works of art. They were the gift of Lord Rhondda and suggestions for the subjects were invited from the whole of Wales. Each statue was the work of a different sculptor. It was a 20th century Welsh hero David Lloyd George, then Secretary of State for War, who unveiled the statues on the 27th October, 1916. A large oil painting commemorating this event is one of the features of the Marble Hall.

SOURCE D

(above) The Marble Hall.

SOURCE E

(above) Cardiff City Hall. The building was completed in 1905.

SOURCE F

(right) Two of the eleven statues celebrating the 'Heroes of Wales': Owain Glyndwr and Boadicea. (The other nine heroes were: Dewi Sant, Hywel Dda, Gerald of Wales, Llywelyn ap Gruffydd, Dafydd ap Gwilym, Henry Tudor, William Morgan, William Williams, Pantycelyn and Sir Thomas Picton.)

1 a) By using the statistics in source B draw a bar graph showing the different rates of growth of the chief industrial towns of Wales between 1851 and 1901.
b) Why did Cardiff grow into the industrial capital of Wales?
c) How do the text and sources C, D, E and F suggest that Cardiff had become more than just an industrial capital of Wales?

2 *Interpretations of history*
The eleven statues in Cardiff city hall represent what some Welsh people in 1916 considered to have been Welsh heroes.
a) Explain why you think these eleven figures were chosen as 'Welsh heroes'.
b) What does this tell us about the attitude of Welshmen like Lord Rhondda and Lloyd George to Welsh history?

profile D.A. Thomas

David Alfred Thomas was born at Ysgubor-wen, Aberdare in 1856. He was the fifteenth child of seventeen born to Samuel Thomas, a grocer at Merthyr Tydfil who later turned to prospecting for coal. Coal made the Thomas family their fortune and this wealth enabled the young David Thomas to be privately educated in Bristol and later at Cambridge University where he obtained an MA in 1883. His education enabled him to meet like-minded students who were interested in economics and politics. But most importantly, his wealth and education enabled him to choose his future career – politics.

The Politician

Thomas was aware that to be successful in politics he needed money, so from Cambridge he returned to the family business in South Wales. He studied coal mining at Clydach Vale. His experience at the pit face with working miners convinced him that his future lay with the Liberals whom he saw as the party of social reform. He was also a proud Welsh patriot, keen to achieve some measure of self-rule for Wales. In 1888 he was elected as one of the two MPs for Merthyr Tydfil. He was to represent Merthyr for 21 years until 1909 when he switched to Cardiff. He formed close links with the Welsh Liberals, particularly Lloyd George and Tom Ellis and together they became deeply involved with the *Cymru Fydd* movement which campaigned for home rule. However, he came to resent Lloyd George's influence in the movement and in 1896 Thomas was largely responsible for destroying *Cymru Fydd*. He turned his attention towards obtaining a cabinet post but when the Liberals won the 1906 election the Prime Minister Campbell-Bannerman failed to promote him. The angry Thomas turned his back on politics.

Captain of Industry

Although he remained an MP after 1906 Thomas devoted his time and energy to building his business empire. He was determined to become the most successful industrialist in South Wales and by 1908 he had established the Cambrian Coal Combine, a company worth £2 million. But the unions resented his refusal to discuss pay and conditions for his workers and he was accused of **profiteering**. His decision to sack 900 miners in the Rhondda was partly responsible for the riots that followed in Tonypandy.

As a businessman Thomas was highly successful and by the beginning of the Great War he was among the richest and most influential of the industrial 'kings' of Wales. His former political ally Lloyd George was so impressed that in 1915 he asked Thomas to represent British industry in America. His success there convinced Lloyd George, now Prime Minister,

SOURCE A

'A Giant at Play', published in the *Western Mail*. The 'cat' represents D.A. Thomas and the 'mouse' the mining unions.

that Thomas's talents could be put to use during the war. He was honoured with the title of Baron Rhondda in 1916 and invited to join the Cabinet as president of the Local Government Board. His greatest achievement came in June 1917 when, as the newly appointed Government Controller of Food, Thomas introduced rationing to solve the food crisis caused by the war. It was a massive success. Worn out by his duties and responsibilities he died at his home at Llanwern in July 1918.

> **I have provided men with the means to pay for the food and clothing of themselves and their families ... By increasing the means of the people I have contributed more to the material happiness and wellbeing of Welsh colliery workers and their families than ... all the miners' leaders combined ... Believe me, I am not out for the accumulation of wealth for its own sake ... The only value of wealth is the influence and power it places in the hands of its possessor to do good.**

SOURCE B

D. A. Thomas, quoted in *The South Wales Daily News* (1916).

> ...the brute insensitivity of coalowners who built up such companies as D. A. Thomas's Cambrian Combine ... and who refused to advance wages and paid no attention to minimum safety regulations.

SOURCE C

Adapted from K. Morgan, *Rebirth of a Nation, Wales 1880–1980* (1981).

> Lord Rhondda, when he was appointed, in 1917, president of the Local Government Board, had to retire from the Directorates of more than thirty Coal, Iron, Steel, Shipping and Railway Companies. His interests were world-wide ... He held large coal properties in the USA ... and Canada. He was the owner of the famous ... historic Llanwern House near Newport ... the ownership of which made him the largest landowner in Monmouthshire, with the exception of Lord Tredegar.

SOURCE D

G. Harvey, ***Capitalism*** *in the South Wales Coalfield* (1918).

> **Let me say this of Lord Rhondda's rationing system: that it abolished queues. It so distributed food that there was no difference between the rich and the poor. The Germans themselves ... called attention to the system in Britain, and pointed out how superior it was to their system. It was a system, let me say, for which Lord Rhondda gave his life. I am glad he saw the success of the efforts for which he had paid such a sacrifice, and that he received the gratitude that was his due...**

SOURCE E

Lloyd George's tribute to Lord Rhondda given in a speech at Leeds (1918).

1 a) What message about D.A. Thomas is the cartoon (source A) trying to convey?

b) How do sources B and C contradict each other? How would you explain this contradiction?

2 In 1916 D. A. Thomas was honoured for his work and achievements by being made Baron Rhondda and given a seat in the House of Lords. What, in your opinion, were his achievements and did they justify the honour he received?

3 *Interpretations of history*
Three biographies have been written about the life of Lord Rhondda in 1918, 1921 and 1937, but there has been nothing since. Why do you think this is so?
Give reasons for your answer.

Trade Unions and Industrial Unrest

For the mass of the workforce there was no golden age of Welsh heavy industry. In Victorian Britain the majority of the working-class people were resigned to social inequality. They even accepted the often harsh treatment that was often dealt out by hard employers. But they were becoming less prepared to suffer wage cuts and unemployment.

The growth of the trade unions led to the growth of the Labour movement which in turn led to greater industrial militancy. For the trade unions and their members the period before the Great War saw many bitter industrial disputes.

Industrial Confrontation 1910–14

In the four years before the outbreak of war Britain was hit by a crippling wave of strikes. The most immediate cause of this industrial unrest was the rise in unemployment, due largely to foreign competition. Many British employers decided it was easier to cut jobs in order to cut costs rather than invest in new technology to become more competitive. Some employers were accused of putting profits before the lives of their employees by cutting safety standards. Whether this was true or not, when disasters happened (as at Senghennydd in 1913 when 439 miners lost their lives in a pit explosion) workers and their unions clashed with owners.

The first area to be hit by strikes was South Wales. During October and November 1910 nearly 30,000 Welsh miners went on strike in search of secure and safer employment and protection of their wages. Coalowners like D.A. Thomas attempted to break the strike by bringing in **blackleg** labour. This led to violence and the army was called in to restore order. The strike lasted eight months after which the defeated miners returned to work. In 1911 the newly formed National Union of Railwaymen called its members out on strike. Troops were again called in and in one incident in South Wales two strikers were shot dead.

Although some employers were prepared to give in to the demands of their workers to settle disputes, others, supported by the government, refused. So in 1912 the Miners Federation organised the biggest strike in its history when over 1 million of its members came out in support of a minimum wage. Soon the dockers of the National Transport Workers Federation and railwaymen joined them and this 'Triple Alliance' of powerful unions brought the country to a standstill. The strike ended when the government agreed to a minimum wage.

The outbreak of war in 1914 put an end to most industrial disputes. During the war both government and unions worked well together. However, the exceptions to this were the miners of South Wales in 1915 and the shipworkers of Clydeside in Scotland who continued to strike during the war. The British press called them traitors for betraying their country in its hour of need.

A modern artist's impression of the bitterness caused by the Taff Vale strike 1901. The sign in the window reads 'There is no traitor in this house'.

SOURCE B

In England the most bitter disputes occurred at Durham, Salford and Liverpool. In this photograph troops are sent in to deal with striking railwaymen in Liverpool (1910–11).

SOURCE C

In 1912 the leaflet on the right was printed by striking workers and circulated amongst the soldiers. Those responsible for the leaflet were arrested, tried and sent to prison.

Don't shoot.
You are Working Men's sons.
When we go on strike to better Our lot which is the lot also of Your Fathers,
Mothers, Brothers and Sisters. *You* are called upon by your officers to *Murder Us.*
Don't do it...
Don't you know that when you are out of the [army] and become a [civilian] again, that You, like us, may be on strike, and You, like us, may be liable to be Murdered by other soldiers.
Boys, Don't Do It;
'Thou shalt not Kill', says the Book.
Don't forget that.
It does not say, 'unless you have a uniform on'.
No. Murder is Murder...
Think things out and refuse any longer to Murder Your [brothers].
Help us to win back Britain for the British and the World for the Workers.

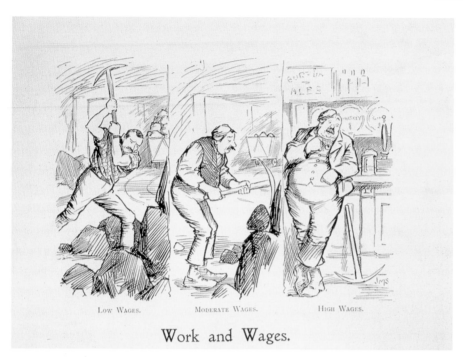

Low Wages.   Moderate Wages.   High Wages.

Work and Wages.

SOURCE D

A cartoon published in the *Western Mail,* March, 1902.

From 1915 onwards South Wales became one of the main centres of anti-war activity in Britain and, despite the best patriotic efforts of the South Wales Miners' Federation, leadership the miners of South Wales became even more ... militant, as the strike of 1915 and the eventual 'taking over' of the coalfield by the government show.

SOURCE E

An extract from HTV's document pack 'The Dragon has Two Tongues' (1984).

SOURCE F

British troops in Mountain Ash (1915). The British army was given the task of restoring order after violent clashes between striking miners and police.

1 a) **What caused the industrial disputes in Wales and England between 1910–14?**
   b) **How and why did the majority of them come to an end?**

2 **In 1910–12 the majority of Britons had been against the use of troops to break up a strike, but in 1915 they supported the use of troops against the miners of South Wales.**

How would you explain this change in British public opinion?

3 **How helpful are the sources in contributing to an understanding of contemporary attitudes towards industrial disputes? Give examples.**

FOCUS

Tonypandy, 1910

On 7 and 8 November 1910 the village of Tonypandy in the Rhondda was the scene of a riot by striking miners. Although there were riots elsewhere in South Wales during 1910–11, it is the riot at Tonypandy that is best remembered today. To socialists it became a legend in the history of the Labour movement in Wales, the spark that set the cause of industrial reform alight in the valleys. To others Tonypandy represents the ruthlessness of an English government who used British soldiers armed with rifles and bayonets against unarmed miners. Others see it as mob rule by greedy and unlawful thugs out to cause havoc. The truth of what happened at Tonypandy is still debated today.

SOURCE A

(right) An extract from the South Wales miners' leader Arthur Horner's autobiography *Incorrigible Rebel* (1960).

I walked over the mountains [from Merthyr Tydfil] through the night to Tonypandy in November 1910 when we heard that Winston Churchill had called out the troops against the miners. The Tonypandy incident followed the strike of 15,000 men employed in the Cambrian group of pits against the scandalous ... subsistence wage.

When I reached Tonypandy the rioting had been going on all through the night. All the shop fronts were smashed. It had begun after the owners had attempted ... to bring blackleg labour to man [the] colliery. I saw in action that day the vicious alliance of the government and the coal owners backed by police and armed troops, against miners who asked no more than a wage little over starvation level. I never forgot that lesson.

SOURCE B

(below) David Evans, was sponsored by the owners of the Cambrian Coal Company to write his book *Labour Strife in the South Wales Coalfield 1910–11* (1911).

In their flight from Llwynypia, and under the impression that the victorious police were still at their heels, the rioters, desperate at the defeat of their plans to take the colliery, gave vent to their rage by smashing the windows of every shop that came within reach.

SOURCE C

(above) 'Dangerous diseases and drastic remedies.' An illustration in the *Western Mail* 9 November 1910.

Investigations on the spot convinced me that the original reports regarding the attacks on the mines on November 8th had been exaggerated [by the police]. What were described as 'desperate attempts' to sack [vandalise] the colliery at Llwynypia proved to have been an attempt to force the gateway ... and a good deal of stone throwing.

SOURCE D

General Macready, the officer commanding the troops in the Rhondda, recalls the riots in *Annals of an Active Life* (1924).

All the Cambrian collieries menaced last night. The Llwynypia Colliery savagely attacked by a large crowd of strikers. Many casualties on both sides. Am expecting two companies of infantry and 200 cavalry today ... Position grave.

SOURCE E

A telegram from Mr Lindsay, Chief Constable of Glamorgan, to Winston Churchill at the Home Office, 10 am, 8 November 1910.

Your request for military. Infantry should not be used till all other means have failed. General Macready will command the military ... [who] will not however be available unless it is clear that the police reinforcements are unable to cope with the situation.

SOURCE F

A telegram from Churchill to the Chief Constable, Mr Lindsay, 1.30 pm, 8 November 1910.

As the situation appears to have become more serious you should, if the Chief Constable ... desires it, move all cavalry into the disturbed district without delay.

SOURCE G

A telegram from Churchill to Macready, 8.10 pm, 8 November 1910.

When I was Home Secretary in 1910, I had a great horror and fear of having to become responsible for the military firing on a crowd of rioters or strikers. I was always in sympathy with the miners ... The Chief Constable of Glamorgan sent a request for the ... military and troops ... But here I ... stopped the ... troops and I sent instead 850 Metropolitan police with the sole object of preventing loss of life. The troops were kept in the background and all contact with the rioters was made by our trusted and unarmed London police who charged, not with rifles and bayonets, but with their rolled up mackintoshes. Thus all bloodshed ... was averted. That is the true story of Tonypandy and I hope it may replace in Welsh villages the cruel lie which they have been fed all these long years.

SOURCE H

Winston Churchill speaking in Cardiff on a general election campaign tour in 1950.

1 a) According to source A what caused the riots?
b) Explain the meaning of the illustration in source C.
c) How reliable are sources B and D?
d) In your opinion, was Winston Churchill (source H) telling the truth?

Explain your answer fully by using all the sources.

2 a) Which sources would be most useful to an historian wishing to find the truth of what happened at Tonypandy?
b) In your opinion, who was to blame for the riots at Tonypandy? Explain fully.

UNIT **2**

<small>ECONOMIC DEVELOPMENTS</small>

Rural Wales: Transition and Change

The Wales of 1906 was divided into the industrial areas of the south east and north east, and the greater part of the country which was almost entirely agricultural. The story of Wales during the nineteenth century had been one of transition and change. As industry rose in importance so agriculture declined, populations moved and some towns grew into cities.

The development of towns such as Merthyr, Cardiff, Pontypridd, Wrexham and Swansea, and the opportunities for industrial employment had persuaded many to leave the countryside in search of a different life. This led to rural depopulation which in time affected the culture and language of the people of Wales. Beyond its borders foreigners tended to see and think of Wales only in terms of its coal mines and the Rhondda valley, although Merthyr, Swansea and Cardiff were household names in many parts of the world. The problems of rural Wales – low wages, poverty and unemployment – were hidden from view and easily forgotten.

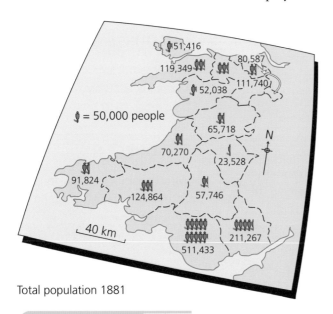

Total population 1881

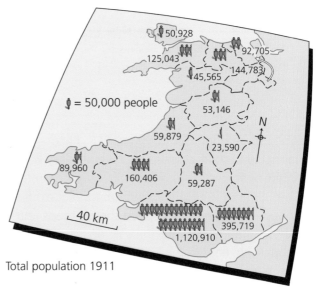

Total population 1911

SOURCE A

Population tables adapted from John Williams 'The Move from the Land' in G.E. Jones, *Wales 1880–1914* (1988).

Agricultural Depression

The situation in England was no better. The fall in agricultural prices in the last 25 years of the nineteenth century caused the farming industry to lay off many of its workers. In 1800 around 54 per cent of the population of England and Wales had lived and worked in the countryside but by 1911 this had fallen to just 20 per cent. In 1900 around 9,000 people emigrated to countries in the Empire like Canada, Australia and New Zealand. By 1911 the number had risen to 33,000. By 1914 Britain was importing over 50 per cent of its food, including around 75 per cent of its grain to make bread. The agricultural depression changed rural Wales and England forever.

The wages paid by farmers ... is in the vast majority of cases insufficient [not enough] to maintain a family ... in a state of ... physical [health]. The labourer's life is that of existing not living [being] starved mentally and emotionally ... the sturdy sons of the village have fled, they have left behind the old-men, the lame, the mentally deficient [ill], the vicious, the born-tired.

SOURCE B

(left) An extract from Seebohm Rowntree, *How the Labourer Lives* (1913).

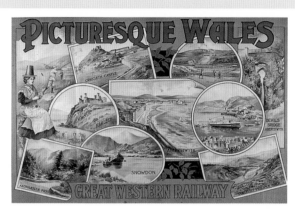

SOURCE C

(left) This advertising poster published by the Great Western Railways appeared in London (c.1909).

We can say that in the year 1912 about one in every fifty of our male agricultural population found their prospects in the United Kingdom so poor that they decided to leave the country altogether. In some parts of the country we find villages from which the majority of the younger able-bodied men have emigrated and it is generally the most capable and energetic who go.

Side by side with emigration for the last thirty years and more, there has been a huge exodus [moving away] of labourers into the large towns where wages are highest. The emigration and migration of the labourers have meant an increasing depopulation of the countryside. The rural exodus is not entirely due to low wages. The fact that the colonial emigration agencies have advertised their own lands ... has ... been an important factor, and so, too, has the general dullness and monotony of life in many of our rural villages. We find that the two [main] causes are, first, the lack of outlook and prospects for the future. Secondly, the low wages and long hours, while the shortage of houses comes next in importance.

SOURCE D

(above) Report of the Land Enquiry Committee (1913).

OVERVIEW

Consider the following key question. To what extent can the period 1906–14 be considered the golden age of Welsh heavy industry?

SOURCE E

(above) Rural labourers at work in the fields (c. 1907).

1 **What use might an historian studying rural change in Wales make of the population tables in source A?**

2 **Why did so many more people leave rural Wales during the period 1885–1914 than in the whole of the previous 50 years? Give reasons for your answer.**

The Great War, 1914–18

> **KEY ISSUE:**
> *What were the effects of the First World War on the people?*

In a city, the name of which few Britons could pronounce (Sarajevo), a foreign prince, of whom even fewer had heard, was murdered by a Serbian in a conflict that was little understood. Yet because of this nearly one million men from the British Empire laid down their lives. What were they fighting for?

Were they fighting for the murdered Crown Prince of Austria-Hungary, Archduke Franz Ferdinand? Were they fighting for the Serbian assassin Gavrilo Princip? Were they fighting for the right of Bosnian-Serbs to be free of Austrian control? Or were they fighting for Belgium? If the average British soldier did not know what he was fighting for; the average British politician did. Britons were fighting for the imperial ambitions of their government, for trade and for the pride of the British Empire. The British people were fed **propaganda** which convinced them that they were going to war to defend their King, country and democracy and to save little countries like Belgium from large bullying states like Germany.

The Alliance System

Between 1900 and 1914, Britain, France and Russia became convinced that Germany wanted to expand at their expense. Germany became convinced that these countries were trying to surround and restrict her.

On 4 August 1914, a little more than a month after the assassination of Franz Ferdinand, Britain declared war on Germany and the Great War began. One of the major factors which had led to war was the alliance system. This meant that when Austria-Hungary declared war on Serbia, Serbia's ally Russia declared war on Austria-Hungary. Austria's ally Germany then declared war on Russia who was joined in the conflict by its ally France. At first, Britain was reluctant to enter the war and only did so when Germany attacked France by going through neutral Belgium.

The World at War

All combatants thought that the war would be over by Christmas 1914, and that no one could stand up to the British Empire and her allies France, Belgium and Russia. But they were wrong. The war carried on and by 1915 it seemed that the whole world was at war. Troops from Australia, Canada, New Zealand, India and South Africa joined the Allies to fight against

Germany, Austria-Hungary and Turkey.

The war was fought mainly in Europe on three fronts: the western front in France and Belgium, the eastern front in Poland and Russia and the southern front in Italy and the Balkans. For the vast majority of Welsh soldiers their war was fought in the British forces against the Germans, in the trenches of the western front (France and Belgium).

TRENCH WARFARE

Within three months of the outbreak of war both sides had reached a stalemate across northern France and Belgium. The soldiers dug themselves into trenches for protection and for much of the next four years that is where they stayed. The area between the trenches of both sides came to be known as 'No Man's Land' or the killing ground. Time after time the generals of both sides ordered mass infantry attacks in the belief that they could break through the lines of trenches and barbed wire. Each time they failed. Massive battles were fought which lasted days, weeks and even months. Some of the better known were Passchendaele, Ypres and the Somme. At the Somme more than 30,000 British soldiers were either killed or wounded in one morning alone in July 1916.

MODERN WEAPONS

Few were prepared for this war, the first modern war in history in which new technology played a major part. Horses were replaced by tanks and trucks, machine guns increased the rate of fire, planes fought duels in the air and ships were sunk by submarines. Mines, grenades and poisoned gas were used for the first time and the countryside was laid waste by millions of tons of high explosive shells fired by thousands of artillery guns. For the 12 million men of all sides who fought on the western front it was a nightmare.

After four years of bitter trench warfare four factors helped break the deadlock in favour of the Allies:

1   By mid-1917 the Allied naval blockade of Germany had almost completely cut off the flow of food and supplies to Germany.
2   The entry of the USA into the war in April 1917 greatly strengthened the Allies.
3   The effective use of new weapons such as the tank enabled the Allies to break through the German lines in 1918.
4   By November 1918 Germany's allies had surrendered.

Crimean War (1854–56)	1,075
Franco-Prussian War (1870–71)	876
Boer War (1899–1902)	10
Balkan War (1912–13)	1,941
Great War (1914–18)	5,509

SOURCE A

The number of men killed per day in the First World War and previous wars, from J. Purnell, *History of the Twentieth Century* (1968).

SOURCE B

A government propaganda poster (1914).

?   1 a) Why was this conflict known as the Great War?
b) In your opinion, what made this war so different from previous wars?
c) What factors eventually enabled the Allies to win the war?

2 a) Why did the government want the British people to believe that they were going to war to defend Belgium?
b) Source B is an example of British propaganda. Explain why, during wartime, propaganda is widely used by all governments.

UNIT

3

Recruitment, Conscription and Objection

Once war had been declared the British government faced a possible crisis. They did not have enough men. Compared to the regular armies of the continental powers – France, Germany and Russia – the British army was tiny. Being an island with a vast overseas empire, Britain's economic resources instead had been used to build a huge navy, which was the largest in the world in 1914.

The Prime Minister Herbert Asquith acted quickly by appointing Lord Kitchener as Secretary for War. Kitchener was a well-known and highly respected general. He realised that this would be a different kind of war and that it was likely to last three years rather than the three months that everyone else expected. Unlike the rest of Europe, Britain did not have enforced military service, so Kitchener's task was to build a new volunteer army to match that of the Germans.

Recruitment

The government launched a massive publicity campaign to persuade men aged between 19 and 35 to join the army and navy. Advertisements appeared in local and national newspapers, recruiting posters were put up everywhere and recruiting meetings were held in village and church halls across the country. The government persuaded churches and chapels to preach that the war was a crusade against evil and that their congregations should join up. Some priests and ministers refused to do this but many others did so willingly. Even the *Eisteddfod* was used to recruit for the war.

SOURCE A

The *Daily Sketch*, 9 January 1915.

RECORD OF GERMAN ATROCITIES CONTINUES TO GROW.

FLAMING RECORD OF GERMAN CRIME.

Damning Proofs Of Atrocities In Belgium And France.

TORTURE BEFORE DEATH.

3,000 People Slaughtered In The Province Of Namur.

HEROD AT DINANT.

31 Children Among 700 Innocent Victims Of The Kaiser.

The Commission of Inquiry into German atrocities in Belgium reports on the Province of Namur that of

Three Hundred Thousand Inhabitants

the Germans have killed

Over Three Thousand.

At Dinant alone seven hundred were killed, including seventy-one women and thirty-one children under fifteen years of age.

Cardinal Mercier's bitter cry against the barbarous persecution of his country is more than justified by the terrible story of slaughter, and worse things even than slaughter, told by

RING OF ENEMIES CLOSING ROUND GERMANY.

The diplomatic mistakes of Germany and her partner Austria threaten to bring them new enemies into the field.

Cardinal Mercier's arrest has caused resentment in Austria as well as in the Catholic parts of the German Empire, and in countries hitherto neutral.

A second and worse mistake has been made by the Commander-in-Chief of the Austrian Navy in deliberately insulting neutral Italy.

The result is that while the two Germanic partners are threatened by fresh dangers they are in peril of quarrelling among themselves.

It is believed in Paris that Austria is considering a separate peace.

The defeats of Turkey have still further complicated the outlook.

A short list of those antagonised by German mistakes or misfortunes is:—

The POPE, who is taking steps to protest against the arrest of Cardinal Mercier;
ITALY, irritated by Austrian threats and the arrest of the Cardinal;
RUMANIA, urged forward by national aspirations to a "Greater Rumania";
BULGARIA, which has cut adrift from German tutelage and is coming to an understanding with Rumania;
GREECE, which has always sympathised with Serbia;
AUSTRIA, which no longer hopes for any glory from the war;
TURKISH POPULACE, angered at their betrayal by the Germans.

The only important news of the fighting is that the French have made more conquests in Alsace.

SHOULDER DEEP IN MUD.

Worse And Worse Conditions In Trenches Of Northern France.

French Official News.

PARIS, 3 p.m., Friday.

Belgium and Northern France.

The enemy's artillery throughout yesterday displayed much activity in Belgium and in the region

AMAZING BLUNDER BY AUSTRIAN ADMIRAL.

"Fleet Must Be Kept To Destroy Italian Navy."

STILL MAKING ENEMIES.

Dangerous Outlook For Germans In South-East Europe.

Another amazing mistake has been made by our enemies.

Admiral Montecuccoli, Commander-in-Chief of the Austro-Hungarian Navy and formerly Minister of Marine, declares that the Austrian Fleet will never accept a challenge from the Anglo-French Fleet, because the Austrian Fleet must be preserved intact to destroy the Italian Fleet. "Our country has need of a second victory of Lissa. It can only obtain it against Italy."

The Austrian Fleet is at present "bottled up" in Pola Harbour, at the head of the Adriatic, where it is watched by a combined British and French squadron.

The Admiral's references to Italy are extraordinarily undiplomatic, because—

Italy has preserved a scrupulous neutrality since the beginning of the war;
Prince von Buelow is at the present moment in Rome on a special mission intended to win over Italian feeling to Germany;
in spite of these efforts a large number of Italians are in favour of intervention in the war on the side of the Allies;

SOURCE B

Recruiting posters from 1914 *(left)* and 1915 *(right)*.

At Bangor in 1915 Lloyd George was allowed to address the *Eisteddfod* audience in the main pavilion.

Thousands of ordinary men from all parts of the country volunteered and so great was the demand to join up that some recruiting offices had to close down temporarily.

A popular method of encouraging recruits was the 'Pals battalions' which were composed of men who joined up together and who came from the same town, village or workplace. In September 1915, 1,000 men from the Lancashire glass-making town of St Helens volunteered. The St Helens Pals consisted of coalminers, office clerks, railwaymen and glass factory workers.

1914	
August	300,000
September	450,000
October	137,000
November	170,000
December	117,000
1914 Total	1,174,000 Average monthly recruitment figure 234,800
1915 Total	1,278,000 Average monthly recruitment figure 106,500

SOURCE C

Recruitment figures published by the War Office (1923).

In the British Empire volunteers streamed into the recruiting centres for the usual mix of reasons: the glamour of a uniform, the prospect of steady pay and escape from [boredom and] out of loyalty to their community, nation and Empire. But the key to mobilisation in 1914 lies in one simple word: duty.

SOURCE D

J.M. Winter, *World War One* (1993).

Conscription

By 1916 the government was again running short of men. The numbers killed and wounded in the war were far higher than anyone had expected. As news of the terrible slaughter reached Britain, enthusiasm for the war began to fade. Young men were reluctant to enlist and the government

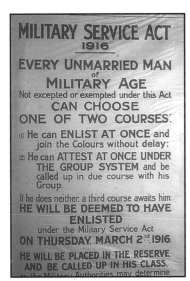

SOURCE E

A poster declaring the Military Service Act (1916).

turned to compulsory military service or **conscription**. In 1916 the Military Service Act was passed which ended voluntary recruitment. Conscription was not popular.

'UNFIT FOR DUTY'

One of the major problems facing the government was that many of the recruits and conscripts were suffering from ill-health and were unfit for military service. Although stricter medicals were introduced after conscription in 1916 the problem was never solved. Of the 2.4 million men called up for war service in 1917–18 nearly 40 per cent of them were declared unfit for frontline duty. The health and social problems of Edwardian Britain had come back to haunt the politicians.

Objection

A number of Britons had opposed the war from the beginning. In 1914 an organisation called the Union of Democratic Control (UDC) was set up to make sure that the errors that had led to the war would never be repeated. A prominent member of the UDC, the Labour politician Ramsay MacDonald, called for diplomacy or discussion rather than fighting to end the war. Supporters of the UDC came to be called pacifists, a word used for the first time to describe those who believed in peace and not war. In 1916 the No-Conscription Fellowship (NFC) was set up with the slogan '"Thou shalt not kill" means what it says'. Public opinion was hostile to these pacifists and the press referred to them as traitors or cowards.

SOURCE F

An interview in the 1980s with Rhys Edwards about his father, a conscientious objector, from K. Strange, *Wales and the First World War*.

[My father] was transported to Dartmoor Prison. On arrival at Princetown all the conchies [conscientious objectors] were stoned by the local children.

All the conchies were kept apart from the [criminals]. Each had a cell 8 feet by 7 feet on the top landing of the main building where the lunatics were kept. Each weekend all the conchies were locked in their cells at 5pm on Friday and not released until Monday morning in time to go to work. The only thing they were allowed to have in the cells was a Bible. Their food was pushed through a vent in the cell door. While on the moor conchies were not allowed contact with their families, and it was impossible for any member of his family to go to the prison, they were unable to afford the train fare.

Everything was done by the Authorities to break my father's spirit.

SOURCE G

The *South West Leader* (1917).

James Hancock, Tailor, 32, applied on conscientious grounds and said that for thirty years it had been his conviction [belief] that he would not, as a Christian, become a soldier, and he could not ... be armed with any weapon for the taking of human life, as it would be inconsistent, as a Christian, for him to do.

A post-conscription recruiting poster (1916).

PUNISHING OBJECTORS

After conscription was introduced the number of people who objected to the fighting increased. Between 1916 and 1918, 11,500 conscientious objectors were dealt with by the law. Seven thousand objectors refused to fight but agreed to join the army in the ambulance and medical corps. Three thousand refused to join the army but agreed to work for the country at home in industry and on the land. However, 1,500 refused to have anything to do with the war, the army or the country. Many of these were sentenced to five years' imprisonment.

1 a) By comparing the recruiting posters of 1914 and 1915 (source B) and that of 1916 (source H), explain how the government had changed its methods and its message. In your answer, state which of the recruiting posters you regard as the most effective in encouraging British men to volunteer for the army?
b) What effect might the newspaper headlines (source A) have had on the British people?
c) Compare the newspaper headlines (source A) and the official recruiting posters (sources B and H). Which in your view would have been most effective in recruiting soldiers? Explain why.

2 a) Explain why the statistics (source C) might have contributed to the passing of the Military Service Act (source E).
b) Why was conscription unpopular?

3 a) Explain the meaning of 'conscientious objector'.
b) Identify the different types of conscientious objector.
c) Why do you think conscientious objectors were treated so badly by the authorities (source F)?

Wales and the Western Front

The reaction in Wales to the news that war had broken out was mixed. Some saw it as an opportunity to change their lives by leaving the pit or the factory for the glamour of wearing the King's uniform and seeing the world. Others were attracted by the thought of glory and of serving their country. But few of them realised what war meant.

Some thought the war was wrong and they were determined not to fight. At a meeting in Merthyr Tydfil in the autumn of 1914, Keir Hardie's attempts to speak against the war caused a near riot. Well-known poets like T. Parry-Williams of North Wales and D. Gwenallt Jones from South Wales wrote and spoke against the war. Gwenallt was arrested and imprisoned for being a conscientious objector. Below are some extracts that highlight the different attitudes of Welsh people to the war.

SOURCE A

(right) Graham Jones, producer and director of the film *Monument (Cofgolofn)* (about the First World War), quoted in the *Western Mail*, November 1995.

The film commemorates what Welshmen did in the war and the passion in Wales against the war because it was considered an English war. For many Welshmen, seeing the German flag on French soil was like seeing the English flag on Welsh soil.

When my father received his 'Call to the colours' he went on the run, eventually landing up in London. It was not long before the military [police] caught him and returned him to Brecon Barracks. While in Brecon he was forcibly dressed, beaten and treated in a most inhuman manner. He removed the uniform with which they dressed him, only to be chased around Brecon Barracks Square naked by soldiers with fixed bayonets.

SOURCE B

(above) An interview in the 1980s with Rhys Edwards about his father. From K. Strange, *Wales and the First World War*.

It was the urge of the youngsters in those days to back Wales against the enemy. We didn't like the Kaiser [the German King] and his way of doing things.

SOURCE C

(above) An interview in the 1980s with Alf Jackson of Swansea, a soldier in the Welsh Regiment. From K. Strange, *Wales and the First World War*.

	Population Census 1911	Number in the armed forces 1918	Percentage of the total population
Wales	2,025,198	280,000	13.82%
Scotland	4,760,904	620,000	13.02%
Ireland	4,390,198	170,000	3.87%
England	34,045,294	4,530,000	13.31%

SOURCE D

(above) Data from the Census Office and Department of Defence.

FARMERS' SONS IN HIDING

The lord-lieutenant [Sir Watkin Williams Wynn] presided over a meeting of the Montgomeryshire Recruiting Committee at Welshpool on Monday and Mr J.H. Tonge spoke of the reluctance of farmers' sons to join, and said that when he had visited some farmers they told him that if he came again they would shoot him.

Sir Watkin said that he knew that in other places when recruiters had been around, the men had run up into the hills and hidden themselves.

... with loud shouts ... one section of the crowd sang 'God Save our Gracious King'. Then most of the people rose from their chairs and it was impossible [for Hardie] to continue. Within a few minutes a section of the crowd sang 'Rule Britannia'.

SOURCE E

(left) A headline and story in the *Western Mail,* January 1915.

... a great patriot I was, bloody glad to get out of the pit. I thought we would have a good time, have a good adventure, it was supposed to be over by Christmas of 1914, what a joke.

SOURCE G

(above) An interview in the 1980s with a soldier, Oliver Powell of Tredegar. From K. Strange, *Wales and the First World War.*

SOURCE F

(above) Keir Hardie addresses a meeting in Merthyr Tydfil, from the *Aberdare Leader* (September 1915).

SOURCE H

(left) An army recruiting office (1915).

1 Which of the sources suggest that Welshmen joined the army willingly? Explain your choice.

2 Source A is a modern film-maker's impression of the contemporary attitude of Welsh people towards the war. Which of the sources: (i) comes closest in supporting his interpretation (ii) comes closest in disagreeing with his interpretation of how Welsh people felt about the war?

3 a) In your opinion, which is the most reliable source for understanding events in history: (i) a drama (ii) a film or (ii) a documentary? Give reasons for your choice.
b) Having studied all the evidence, do you believe that the views expressed by the film-maker in source A are justified?

UNIT 3

THE FIRST WORLD WAR

Britons at War: Life in the Trenches

(right) A still from the film *Paths of Glory* (1957).

(above) A contemporary photograph of life in the trenches.

> The dead were everywhere ... grim disfigured corpses rotting in the sun, so horrible in their discolour that it called for an act of faith to believe that these were once young men, sent to their [deaths] by their fellow men.

(above) The scene described after an attack through No Man's Land by Welshman Wyn Griffith, a junior officer. From M. Plowman, *A Subaltern on the Somme* (1927).

The men who volunteered and marched to war in 1914 were unprepared for what they were to experience at the front. Thoughts of honour and glory, of cavalry charges and heroic combat were soon forgotten in the mud of deep, often water-filled, rat-infested trenches, surrounded by the rotting bodies of their friends. This was a war unlike any other war before or since.

By the beginning of 1915 the soldiers of both sides had dug themselves into trenches that stretched for over 300 miles from the English Channel to the border of Switzerland. At first the trench was simply a hole dug into the earth. But over time and with experience it became more complicated with dug-outs, firing steps, sand bags and barbed wire. The trench with its dug-out became the home of soldiers in the front line – thousands of them lived and died there.

Life in the trenches soon settled down into a routine of shifts for sentry duty, rest, sleep, meals and fatigues. Almost every night soldiers would be selected for fatigue duty. This involved bringing up supplies of food, medicine, materials for repairing the trench, ammunition and mail from behind the front line. Boredom became a major problem which often led to soldiers being careless and getting shot by German snipers waiting for a man's helmet or head to appear above the trench.

Disease

The trench was an unhealthy place to live. The soldiers found it difficult to keep clean. They were covered by hundreds of lice and surrounded by rats. When it rained it filled the three metres deep trenches so that men were often waist or knee deep in water for days. This often led to flu, pneumonia and bronchitis. A common disease was trench foot which turned the feet green and swollen. The everyday smells of the trenches were foul and in summer the stench of death was so strong that recruits would sometimes pass out when they first arrived.

'Over the top'

Despite all this, the hardships experienced by the men were as nothing compared to the horror and fear of 'going over the top'. This meant leaving the safety of the trench for an attack into No Man's Land. The shared suffering of trench life led to a sense of companionship which was cruelly cut short when the order to attack the enemy was given. In many mass attacks the casualty rate was as high as 40 per cent.

The water through which we waded was alive with swimming frogs. Red slugs crawled up the sides of the trenches, and queer beetles with dangerous looking horns wriggled along dry ledges and invaded the dugouts in search of the vermin which infested them.
Rats were the worst plague. There were thousands of rats in this part of the line and they were [cheeky] devils. In the dugout next door the straw at night writhed with them. Some of them were as big as cats having gorged on [eaten] the corpses.

SOURCE D

Trench life as described by war correspondent Philip Gibbs in his book *Realities of War* (1920).

Soldier A: I thought of all the people that I liked, and things that I wanted to do, and told myself that that was all over, that I had done with that; but I was sick with sorrow all the same.

Soldier B: In about five minutes from now I shall be dead. I envied the people whom I had seen in billets two nights before. They will be alive at dinner time today, and tonight they'll be snug in bed;
but where shall I be? My body will be out there in No Man's Land ...
What is done to people when they die?

SOURCE E

The poet John Masefield recorded the last thoughts of men about to 'go over the top'. From C. Martin, *Battle of the Somme* (1973).

The day has almost dawned when I shall really do my little bit in the cause of civilisation. Tomorrow morning, I shall take my men over the top in the first attack. Should it be God's holy will to call me away, I am quite prepared to go ... I could not wish for a finer death, and you, dear Mother and Dad, will know that I died doing my duty to my God, my country and my King.

SOURCE F

A last letter home by J.S. Engall, a junior officer. From L. Houseman, *War Letters of Fallen Englishmen* (1930).

1 a) **What do sources C, D, E or F, tell you about what life was like for the ordinary soldier at the front?**
b) **How useful are films such as source A to those who wish to study the Great War?**

2 a) **During wartime all governments operate rules of censorship, which means that no one is allowed to criticise the army, government or conduct of the war. Explain why you think they did this?**

b) **Under the rules of censorship all private letters sent by British soldiers back home were read by a special team of officers or censors before being sent to their destinations. Some letters were never sent on. Why might a censor object to source D but approve of source E? Explain your answer.**

3 **Write an essay of no less than 250 words describing daily life in the trenches.**

UNIT 3

THE FIRST WORLD WAR

The Impact of War on Civilian Life

SOURCE A

A government propaganda
poster (1915).

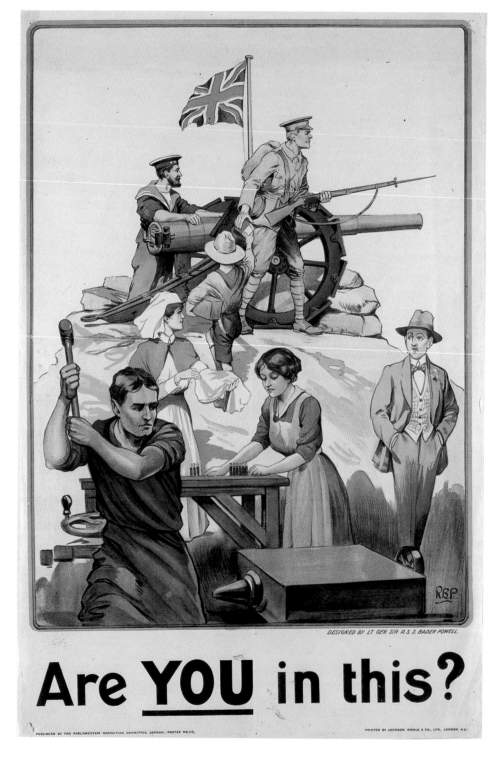

The impact of total war was to change Wales and Britain forever. The whole nation was mobilised for the war effort by a government determined to control every aspect of life on the home front. In August 1914 Parliament passed the Defence of the Realm Act (DORA) which gave it the power to ban, restrict or censor anything that it thought could harm the war effort. Newspapers were first to be affected by the new censorship laws, followed by advertising posters. Soon government propaganda was everywhere. DORA enabled the state to control shipping and shipbuilding, engineering, agriculture, railways and the mines. Under the newly created Ministry of Munitions the government took charge of industrial production and supply. This enabled it to control prices and profits. Total war came to mean total state control.

There were benefits for the British public. Lloyd George believed that warfare and welfare went hand in hand and when he became Prime Minister in 1916 he set about improving the lives of ordinary citizens. The government began to fund organisations like the Burry Port Garden Suburb Company, which built homes with cheap rents for workers at the Pembrey munitions factory near Llanelli. State education, health and hospital care steadily improved. Wages for industrial and agricultural workers also went up but only in return for a promise not to strike.

Daily Life

At first life at home did not change that much. However, as the war continued its effects became harder to ignore. Housewives were among the first to notice the massive price rises and shortages of some foods in the shops. This was due partly to inflation but also to German submarines or U-Boats which were sinking hundreds of merchant ships bringing food and raw materials to Britain. The government used its powers under DORA to make waste illegal. In one instance, this led to a Welsh housewife being fined £20 for feeding meat to her dog. The situation had become so serious that in January 1918 rationing for essential foodstuffs was introduced.

The government was spending nearly £5.5 million a day on the war. To avoid going bankrupt it increased income tax from 6p in the pound in 1914 to 30p by 1918. People were encouraged to spend less and save more and to use these savings to buy war bonds from the government to help pay for the war. In return the government promised to pay the money back, with interest, once the war was over.

Changes in Agriculture

For the tenant farmers of Wales the war brought change and prosperity. The demand for milk and other dairy products, livestock and corn increased. They were helped by bodies such as the Welsh Council of Agriculture and the 70 Agricultural Organisation Societies which offered advice and technical assistance. By passing the Corn Production Act of 1917 the government tried to encourage greater efficiency in the production of important foods by guaranteeing farmers a fixed price. Even agricultural labourers were guaranteed a minimum wage which brought them economic security for the first time.

SOURCE B

Government advertising posters (1915–17).

However, not everyone benefited. Rich landowners saw the value of their large estates decline because of increased taxation and inflation. From 1917 some estates which had been in existence for a century and more were broken up and sold off to their ex-tenant farmers. The Talbot estate of Margam, the Hanbury estate of Pontypool Park in South Wales and the Glynllifon and Bodelwyddan estates in the north were among the first to be sold off.

Changes in Industry

Some historians have suggested that the Great War caused a second industrial revolution. The size of factories and the number of industrial workers employed in them increased significantly. They turned away from producing consumer goods towards the mass production of war materials. The Welsh coal and steel industries received a huge boost as demand outstripped supply. Welsh coal was needed to power the Allied navies and to generate the energy needed by British and French industry. Welsh steel was used to build the first tanks.

Soon some workers, such as the miners, came to realise how important their industry was for the war effort. They began to ask for better working conditions and higher wages. The Liberal government had little choice but to discuss terms, but the two sides failed to agree. In the summer of 1915 the miners' union, the South Wales Miners Federation, called its members out on strike. There was an outcry in the country against the Welsh miners who were soon joined by Scottish shipworkers on Clydeside. The headline of a London newspaper, the *Evening Standard*, read 'Germany's Allies in Wales'. The strike came to an end when Lloyd George met the miners' union officials in Cardiff and gave in to their demands.

Women at War

One of the greatest changes in Britain caused by the war concerned the role and status of women. When war broke out the Suffragettes and the Liberal government buried their differences. Both were determined to work together to ensure victory. As Minister of **Munitions** Lloyd George was first to realise the impact war would have at home. With thousands of men volunteering to fight at the front, who would work in the war factories? In July 1915, when the Suffragette leader Mrs Emmeline Pankhurst led a march of 30,000 women through London demanding the 'Right to Serve'; the government supported her. Soon Lloyd George was employing increasing numbers of women in the munitions factories and between July 1915 and July 1918 their numbers rose from 255,000 to 948,000. This was dirty, dangerous work. The hours were long and the pay poor but the munitionettes (as they were called) worked hard to increase the production of bullets and shells. They were inspired by the propaganda posters which said 'Women's battle cry is work, work, work' and 'Shells made by women may save their husbands' lives'. Unfortunately, not everything changed: in spite of Lloyd George's promises of a fair minimum wage, women factory workers were paid about half (£2.20 per week) that received by men (£4.32).

By 1918 women were employed in a variety of jobs and a soldier returning from the front would have noticed the huge difference. There were women train station porters, railway ticket collectors, bus-conductors, policewomen, postwomen, drivers and even grave-diggers. Although when men returned at the end of the war many women were forced to give up their jobs, they had proved themselves, according to Herbert Asquith, 'to be as active and as efficient as men'. As a reward for loyal service the Prime Minister Lloyd George passed a law in 1918 giving women over 30 years of age the right to vote and to stand for election as an MP. What the Suffragette Movement had failed to achieve in 50 years was largely achieved in the four years of war.

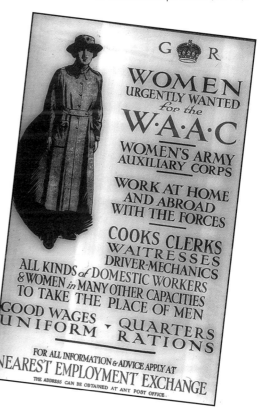

> We want to help Britain even though it is governed by Mr Asquith and his Liberals. We should rally to the country, not the government. It is a thousand times more the duty of Suffragettes to fight the Kaiser for the sake of liberty than it is to fight anti-suffrage governments.

SOURCE D

(left) An extract from a speech by Mrs Pankhurst in 1914.

?

1 Under the following headings, describe the changes which took place in Britain during the Great War: (i) social changes (ii) economic changes and (iii) political changes.

2 a) Explain what you believe to be the message of the poster in source A.
b) Read source D. Which of the propaganda posters might Mrs Pankhurst not approve of? Explain why.
c) Was the Defence of the Realm Act (DORA) necessary? Explain your answer.

THE FIRST WORLD WAR

'The war to end all wars': A Welshman at the Paris Peace Conference

On 11 November 1918 the First World War came to an end. A near defeated Germany agreed to sign a truce, or armistice in return for a just peace. The Prime Minister of Britain, David Lloyd George, intended to honour his promise of a fair treaty. However, at the peace conference at Versailles near Paris he was opposed by the French Prime Minister Georges Clemenceau, nicknamed the Tiger, who wanted revenge and compensation. Lloyd George was supported by the American President Woodrow Wilson who had drawn up a list of 14 points designed to establish a lasting peace. Unfortunately, some of his points upset both Lloyd George and Clemenceau. The three leaders – known as the Big Three – could not agree on how best to deal with Germany.

SOURCE A

A cartoon published in 1919. The figures represent the Allied leaders at Versailles:
(1) Clemenceau of France,
(2) Wilson of the USA and
(3) Lloyd George of Britain.
The child represents the future adult of 1940, weeping in the corner.

PEACE AND FUTURE CANNON FODDER

The Tiger: *"Curious! I seem to hear a child weeping!"*

After six months of hard bargaining the Treaty of Versailles was signed. Expectations for establishing permanent world peace had been high. But the treaty was a compromise peace which pleased no one least of all the Germans who were not allowed to attend the peace conference.

The Attitude of the British People

The attitude of the British people had changed in the four years since the beginning of the war in 1914. The loss of nearly 1 million men dead and

J.A. Hooper:	Towards the end of the war, we were so fed up we wouldn't even sing 'God Save the King' on church parade. Never mind the bloody King we used to say, he was safe enough; it should have been God save us....'
L. Jessop:	By the end of 1917 we couldn't care less who won as long as we could get the war over.

SOURCE B

(left) Extracts from interviews with former soldiers quoted in M. Middlebrook, *The First Day of the Somme* (1971).

over 2 million seriously injured caused much anger and bitterness. To the average British family these statistics meant little. To them the casualties of war meant the loss of a father, a son, a brother or a cousin; few families were left untouched by the war. In 1918 people were hardly in the mood to forgive and forget. Like the French, they wanted Germany harshly punished and forced to accept the blame for starting the war. This placed Lloyd George in a difficult position. The British people had re-elected him in 1918 to the chants and slogans of 'Hang the Kaiser' and 'Squeeze the German lemon until the pips squeak'. He hoped that with the war over the people would begin to put away their hatred and resentment, but he was wrong. In order to survive politically he had to be harder on the Germans than he wanted to be. This led to a harsher treaty which in turn led to German resentment and the desire for revenge.

SOURCE C

(above) A British propaganda poster issued by the government in 1916.

SOURCE D

(left) One of the hundreds of war cemeteries set up in Belgium and France. This one at Passchendaele contains the bodies of British soldiers killed in the area.

1 a) **Describe the attitude of: i) the British civilians at home and ii) the British soldiers at the front towards the Germans at the end of the war. Refer to the previous chapter.**
   b) **Explain why their attitudes were so different.**

2 a) **Explain why propaganda posters such as source C were: (i) successful in helping Lloyd George to win the war and (ii) causing Lloyd George problems in making the peace?**
   b) **Re-write source C as a propaganda poster giving the German point of view.**
   c) **What does this exercise tell us about the nature of wartime propaganda?**

David Lloyd George

A photograph of Lloyd George

SOURCE A

(right) Adapted from Gwynfor Evans, *Welsh Nation Builders* (1988).

Early Life

David Lloyd George was born in Manchester in 1863 where his Pembrokeshire-born father was a teacher. Within two years his father had died and Lloyd George, his brother and mother returned to live in Wales. They lived with his mother's brother Richard Lloyd, a shoemaker from Llanystumdwy near Cricieth, North Wales. Source A describes the early influences on his life.

> Richard Lloyd ... was a remarkable man, a cultured and strong minded cobbler who greatly influenced his nephew. It was a time of dramatic social and industrial change; railways and the English press spread through the country; in the rural areas the conflict between landlord and tenant resulted in the tenant throwing off the power of the anglicised landed families. L.G. was seven when English education was imposed on all Welsh children; he was twenty-one when household suffrage was extended to rural constituencies, and in five years' time county councils were established. A new middle class emerged, and L.G., the solicitor from the humble shoemaker's home, became a part of it.

The Young MP

The young Lloyd George was a Welsh-speaking nationalist and a radical. He became a solicitor and in 1890 he was elected as the Liberal MP for the Caernarfon Boroughs. He was greatly influenced by a fellow Welshman and Liberal Tom Ellis, the son of a tenant farmer and MP for Merionethshire. Together they fought for the cause of Welsh nationalism and for social and political equality and justice.

Cabinet Minister

After the death of his friend Tom Ellis in 1899 Lloyd George turned his attention away from purely Welsh affairs and concentrated on foreign policy issues such as the Boer War (1899–1902). He believed that the war against the Boer or Dutch settlers of South Africa was wrong and he openly campaigned against it. This made him very unpopular and he was accused of being unpatriotic. On one occasion in 1901 he was forced to escape from an angry mob at Birmingham Town Hall disguised as a policeman.

After the Liberal election victory of 1906 Lloyd George was given his first cabinet post when he joined the government as the President of the Board of Trade. He was promoted to Chancellor of the Exchequer when Asquith

THE ARCH-DRUID OF DOWNING STREET.

SOURCE B

A cartoon of Lloyd George from *Punch* (1910).

became leader of the party in 1908. As Chancellor Lloyd George had the power to force through radical social reforms such as old age pensions, labour exchanges for the unemployed and a health insurance scheme for workers. These costly reforms brought him into conflict with the Conservatives and their wealthy supporters who objected to having to pay for them. But Lloyd George won the fight.

Thirty years after the National Health Insurance Act was passed men who were drawing their sickness or unemployment pay would still speak of 'being on Lloyd George'. This is perhaps a better tribute to him than all the books about him which stand on library shelves.

SOURCE C

E. Nash and A. Newth, *Britain in the Modern World: The Twentieth Century* (1967).

The Great War

At first Lloyd George opposed the war but when he saw that there was no alternative he threw himself into the conflict. In 1915 he was appointed Minister of Munitions with the task of increasing the production of weapons and of ensuring that they were delivered to the army and navy as speedily as possible. His success paved the way for his appointment in 1916 as Prime Minister. Inspired by Lloyd George's energetic leadership the British people came through the war which eventually ended in an Allied victory. At the Paris Peace Conference in 1919 Lloyd George showed that he had become a world statesman with the ability to deal with difficult international issues.

Prime Minister

During the war Lloyd George had led a **coalition** government of Liberals and Conservatives and for four years after his election victory in 1918 the majority remained loyal to him. He was popular and respected as 'the man who won the war'. However, his time as a post-war Prime Minister was not a happy one. His quarrel with Asquith led to the Liberal Party being split in two, which virtually destroyed it. This meant that the majority of Lloyd George's coalition government was Conservative rather than Liberal. Some Conservatives did not trust him. They had never forgiven Lloyd George for defeating the House of Lords over the People's Budget in 1909 and again in 1911.

SOURCE D

An extract from the *Caernarvon and Denbigh Herald,* August 1915.

It was the new Lloyd George shells [bombs] which gave us the heart to make the charge, after being so heavily hit. These new shells are magnificent and after our fellows got into the captured trenches they gave three cheers for Lloyd George.

DELIVERING THE GOODS.

SOURCE E

A cartoon from *Punch*, April 1915.

Within two years of the end of the war Lloyd George was faced by an economic slump, rising unemployment and a civil war in Ireland. He wished to continue his social reforms but the country could not afford them and the Conservatives disliked them. Reluctantly he had to cut the government's budget by £75 million. Added to this were the several scandals in which he was involved. The most serious of these was the accusation of selling titles to boost his party's funds: a knighthood, for example, was said to cost £15,000. By 1922 some Conservatives believed that it was time to end the coalition. Led by the leader of the Conservative Party Bonar Law, they turned on Lloyd George and forced him to resign. The King, George V, said, 'He will be Prime Minister again.' He was wrong. Lloyd George never again held government office. He died in 1945. Churchill said of him, 'he was the greatest master of the art of getting things done and putting things through that I ever knew'.

His lifetime had spanned 80 of the most eventful years in British history. During those years, his career had taken him from a small solicitor's office in Cricieth to the House of Commons and to 10, Downing Street.

Today, historians still argue furiously about his qualities and his importance ... He may have been the 'rogue [mad] elephant among British Prime Ministers', he was a great leader and opportunist. He never forgot the class and the people from which he sprang.

SOURCE F

(left) David Evans, *Wales in Modern Times* (1979).

(above) Lloyd George pictured with Hitler at Berchtesgaden in Germany (1936).

(above) Lloyd George pictured at the chairing of the Bard ceremony at the 1926 Swansea National *Eisteddfod*.

1 a) How far was Lloyd George as a politician influenced by the experiences of his early life?
b) What images of Lloyd George are the *Punch* cartoons (sources B and E) trying to convey to its readers? By using the text and sources in this and in other chapters, write: (i) a character study of Lloyd George and (ii) list his achievements and failures.

2 In your opinion, does Lloyd George deserve to be remembered as a great wartime leader or a peacetime social reformer? Explain your choice.

UNIT

THE FIRST WORLD WAR

'A land fit for heroes': Britain 1919–22

> I have today given two minutes praying for our dead and two hours regretting I am not one of them ... They 'live' in a world where no bread is needed; I am condemned to exist in a land that threatens to starve me.

SOURCE A

An extract from a letter to *The Times*, 11 November 1919.

The effects of the Great War were to influence British politics for much of the 1920s. In the election of 1918 Lloyd George cashed in on his popularity as 'the man who won the war'. He had campaigned for 'a land fit for heroes'. This raised the expectations of the British people who thought their Prime Minister would also 'win the peace'. However, there were difficulties.

Political Problems

Lloyd George did not have a free hand to put his ideas for social reform into action. The British people had voted for the wartime coalition of Liberals and Conservatives to continue – Lloyd George was its leader but the Conservatives under Bonar Law had a majority in the House of Commons. Lloyd George was forced to modify his social reforms.

Social and Economic Problems

Britain was suffering from a post-war depression. The country had spent £8,752 million on the war. There was a massive increase in the National Debt which meant that 50 per cent of the money raised by taxation went to pay the interest alone. Nearly 40 per cent of British merchant shipping had been lost. Money for the war effort had been taken from social projects like housing with the result that by 1920 about 600,000 new houses were urgently needed.

The war had drained the resources of many foreign countries so that they were buying fewer British goods. Traditional heavy industries like coal, iron and steel were producing too much for the market and employers were forced either to cut wages or reduce the workforce. By the end of 1920 **demobilisation** had added over 4 million men to those already seeking work.

SOCIAL AND INDUSTRIAL UNREST

The slow pace of demobilisation caused resentment among enlisted men. Everyone wanted to go home. It was made worse by the fact that the officers seemed to be given preferential treatment. The result was a series of mutinies in the army and navy. In an effort to calm the situation, the Secretary for War, Winston Churchill, changed the policy to 'first in, first out' to include all ranks.

The trade unions had gained power during the war and they were reluctant to lose it. They were also determined to fight for better working conditions and wage increases for their members. During 1919–20 there were nearly 2,000 strikes. The miners, railwaymen and transport workers again joined together to form the Triple Alliance under the leadership of Ernest Bevin. This proved effective in forcing the government to give in to their demands rather than risk a general strike. However, by 1921 the Triple Alliance had collapsed. The miners were forced back to work after a strike and to accept a cut in wages. At the same time unemployment had risen to over 2 million.

GOVERNMENT CUTS

The advice of the economist J.M. Keynes who suggested increased spending to encourage economic growth was ignored. Instead the government resorted to cutbacks in expenditure. A committee was set up to advise Lloyd George on where these cuts should to be made. The Geddes committee recommended that spending should be cut on public services like education, health and welfare. These cuts in spending and services came to be known as the 'Geddes Axe'. They were deeply unpopular.

SOCIAL REFORMS

Promising 'homes fit for heroes', Lloyd George carried through a building programme for over 200,000 new houses by 1922. He also extended National Insurance to cover a greater proportion of the workforce. This allowed them to claim both sickness and unemployment benefit. It came to be known as the dole. However, rising prices, the deepening depression and opposition from within his own coalition put a stop to any further reforms. Lloyd George's promises had fallen far short of people's expectations.

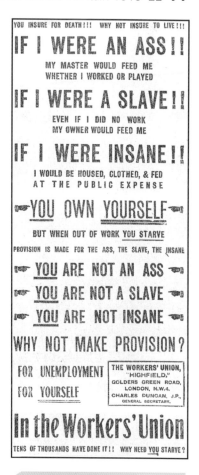

SOURCE B

(above) The *Daily Herald*, 23 December 1920.

More than anything I hated to see war-crippled men standing in the gutter selling matches. We had been promised a land fit for heroes; it took a hero to live in it. I'd never fight for my country again.

SOURCE C

(above) An interview with F.W. Turner, a soldier. From M. Middlebrook, *The First Day of the Somme* (1971).

?

1 a) What do you understand by the statement 'A land fit for heroes'?
b) Using the text and sources identify five features of the post-war depression.

2 What do we learn from sources A, B and C about the feelings of ex-servicemen towards the economic depression?

3 'Lloyd George's promises had fallen far short of people's expectations.' Do you agree or disagree with this statement? Use the text and sources to write an essay explaining your point of view.

OVERVIEW

Consider the following key question. What were the effects of the First World War on the people?

Wales – Language and Identity

UNIT 4

> **KEY ISSUE:**
> *How and why did people's attitudes and values change in the period 1906–19?*

By the end of the Great War some believed that Wales was a nation facing massive problems. Why?

By 1911 the country was divided between the 'Welsh' (native Welsh speakers), 'Anglo-Welsh' (native non-Welsh speakers) and those people who had moved into Wales, who spoke only English. This division of the population contributed to the decline of a sense of 'Welshness', particularly as more and more people began to use the English language. According to one historian, Tim Williams, many Welsh people turned to using English because it was the language of an empire and the emerging democracy in Edwardian Britain. Others argue that the decline in the language was due to the attitude of the government in London towards Wales and the Welsh.

SOURCE A

Adapted from *Welsh Nation Builders* (1988), by Gwynfor Evans, a Welsh nationalist and historian.

History is a nation's memory. A nation [who does not remember] her history is like a person who has lost his memory. A person with no sense of the past is not fully a person, and a nation without a sense of her past is not fully a nation. Welsh people who [do not know] of their nation's history are unlikely to think of Wales as a nation ... and are therefore unlikely to be concerned [about Wales's] future.

SOURCE B

A letter to the Board of Education from the Secretary to the Managers of Briton Ferry National School (1905).

The managers beg to inform you that not having received an application from a single parent to have a child taught Welsh ... the managers think it unwise to introduce Welsh teaching.

SOURCE C

An extract translated from *Oes a Gwaith y Prif Athraw y Parch Michael E. Jones* by E Pan Jones (1903).

... it is the Welsh themselves who are letting English in, and making an effort to turn Welsh out of their families, chapels and trade, and timidly allowing the English to turn it out of our law courts. It is up to the Welsh themselves as to whether Welsh dies or lives, and if it dies the blame will be theirs. Let every Welshman keep his language on the hearth, in chapel and in business and it will live.

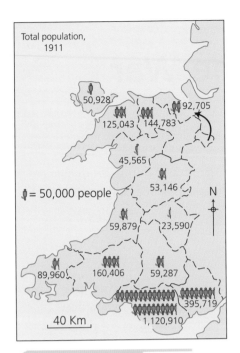

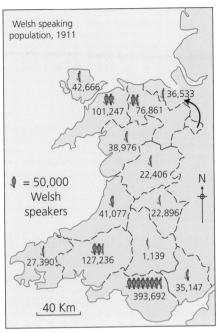

SOURCE D

(above) Two maps showing (i) the total population of Wales in 1911 and (ii) the total Welsh speaking population in 1911. Calculated from census returns.

SOURCE E

(above) An example of the *Welsh Not* (*19th century*) from the Museum of Welsh Life, St Fagans. It was the policy in some schools to punish children for speaking Welsh by forcing them to wear the *Welsh Not* hung around their necks.

We cannot here discuss in detail all the ... factors that have contributed to this steady decline of the Welsh language, Welsh nationalists ... still attribute it to the anti-Welsh policy of the Church, Parliament, and to the English system of education in Wales. It has not been due, they say, to any lack of [interest] among the native population, but to ... the efforts of the English and of English officials in Wales, to suppress it in order to crush the spirit of Welsh nationality.

SOURCE F

(left) J.V. Morgan, an historian, in *The Welsh Mind in Evolution* (1925).

The Welsh were in a minority in Tai-Harry-Blawd, where they were mixed with English, Irish and Scotch people, whose fathers and grandfathers had been brought into Wales by the old Iron Kings. At first I knew only Welsh from my parents ... but as I went on playing with the Scott, Hartley, Ward and McGill children, I became more fluent than in my native language. Dad was annoyed when I started replying in English to what he had said in Welsh, but our Mam said in Welsh: 'Oh, let him alone. What odds, anyway?'

SOURCE G

(left) Jack Jones, a former miner and best-selling novelist from the Rhondda, remembers his childhood in Edwardian Wales. An extract from his autobiographical novel, *Unfinished Journey* (1938).

1 a) Draw a bar graph to show: **(i)** the total population for each county and **(ii)** the Welsh speaking population of each county in 1911.
b) Compare the maps and figures in source D. What percentage of the total population of Wales spoke Welsh in 1911?

2 a) Read the sources and the text. List the factors that were contributing to the decline of the Welsh language.
b) Which of them do you think was most responsible for the decline in the use of Welsh and why?

3 In your opinion, why had people's attitudes towards the language changed by 1911? Explain your answer.

Hedd Wyn and the War Poets

SOURCE A

A photograph of Hedd Wyn

Attitudes to the First World War and the idea of war began to change after 1914. The first signs of this change appeared in the works of the war poets.

The English War Poets

The better-known English war poets were Rupert Brooke, Siegfried Sassoon, Wilfrid Owen and Robert Graves, all of whom were officers. These soldier-poets had been among the first to volunteer for the army. They were young, well-educated men from the English middle class but above all they were idealists. To some of them war meant glory, courage and the opportunity for men of honour to die for what they believed in – for King, Country and the Empire. At first their poems reflected the mood of patriotism and enthusiasm which greeted the outbreak of war in 1914, while they were still ignorant of the horrors of modern war. By 1916, those that had survived began to change their opinions.

SOURCE B

(right) A.J.P. Taylor, *English History 1914–45* (1965).

The early poets, Rupert Brooke ... wrote with an ... innocence which they carried over from peacetime. After the Somme came poets who saw in war only horror and suffering, [except for] the comradeship of the trenches. Most of them remained war poets, [as some called them] anti-war poets. [Siegfried] Sassoon turned against the war altogether, after winning the Military Cross, and claimed to be a conscientious objector. The others still wanted to destroy [the evil of Germany], though they saw this [evil] in their own commanders as well as on the other side. In any case, these poets spoke only for a minority.

SOURCE C

(right) Robert Graves, *Goodbye to All That* (1929).

We decided not to make any public protest against war. Siegfried said that we must 'keep up the good reputation of the poets' – as men of courage he meant. Our best place would be back in France, away from the more shameless madness of home-service. There, our function would be not to kill Germans, though that might happen, but to make things easier for the men under our command.

SOURCE D

(right) K.O. Morgan, *Rebirth of a Nation: Wales, 1880–1980* (1981).

There were no significant war poets [in Wales] of the type of Wilfrid Owen and Siegfried Sassoon in England: Hedd Wyn was recalled as an example of meaningless sacrifice not of national heroism.

Hedd Wyn

Ellis Humphrey Evans was born in 1887 at a farm called Yr Ysgwrn near the village of Trawsfynydd, Merionethshire. He was the eldest of three sons born to poor farmers Evan and Mary Evans. Although he received only a basic education at the local primary and chapel Sunday schools, he was a bright boy who had a particular talent for poetry. He was encouraged by his father, also a self-taught poet, to compete in local *eisteddfodau*. He won the first of his six chairs at Bala in 1907 and he soon gained a reputation for his poetry, being given the bardic name of Hedd Wyn (peace) at another competition in 1910.

Hedd Wyn's attitude to the war was mixed. He did not welcome war but he believed that it was a just war and his poems reflect the optimism felt generally by the British people that they would be victorious. However, his attitude began to change, particularly when the numbers of men from his home district killed on the western front began to rise. Many of them were his friends and neighbours and in honour of their sacrifice he wrote poems of remembrance such as *Nid a'n Ango* (Do Not Forget) and *Rhyfel* (War).

In February 1917 Hedd Wyn enlisted in the army but he did so reluctantly in order to save his 18-year-old brother Bob from being conscripted. He was trained at Litherland near Liverpool where he may have met Robert Graves, a captain in his regiment the Royal Welsh Fusiliers. A fully trained Private, Evans arrived at the front line in France on 9 June. On 31 July at the battle of Pilkem ridge he was mortally wounded and died some hours later in a first aid post. He was one of 31,000 British soldiers killed that day. He once told his fiancée, Jini Owen, that he could never kill a German but that they would have to kill him.

Since October 1916 Hedd Wyn had been working on a poem called *Yr Arwr* (the Hero) which he intended to submit at the Birkenhead *Eisteddfod* of 1917. He finished the poem on 15 July and, with the permission of the army's censors, submitted it for the competition. At the *Eisteddfod* in September the poem and its composer were judged to have won the competition. At the chairing ceremony, attended by Lloyd George, it was announced that he had died five weeks earlier. The chair was draped in black and taken home to Yr Ysgwrn. It became known as the Black Chair of Birkenhead.

SOURCE E

(below) An extract from *Rhyfel*, translated by Hedd Wyn's biographer Alan Llwyd.

> The harps to which we sung are hung
> On willow boughs, and their refrain
> Drowned by the anguish of the young
> Whose blood is mingled with the rain.

SOURCE F

(above) A photograph of the grave of Hedd Wyn.

1 Read sources B and C.
   a) What do you understand by the term 'war poet'?
   b) What did Captain Graves mean by 'the shameless madness of home service'?

2 a) Why did the attitude of men like Graves and Sassoon and Hedd Wyn change towards the war by 1916?
   b) Why might Hedd Wyn's poetry have had a greater impact on the Welsh people than the poetry of men like Graves and Sassoon on the English people?
   c) In your view, did the works of the poets reflect or represent the views of the British public towards the war in 1917?

3 In 1923 a statue was erected in Trawsfynydd to Hedd Wyn where he is shown as a shepherd poet. Why might he have approved of being depicted as a shepherd rather than as a soldier?

Church and Chapel: The Religion of the People

Church

The Church of England or Anglican Church was, by an Act of Parliament, the religion of the state. However, in Wales it was far from popular. It was seen by many as the religion of the middle and wealthy classes – the landowner and the mine owner. With some exceptions, its services were conducted mainly in English. Politically the Church was regarded as being pro-Tory whereas the majority of the Welsh people were pro-Liberal. In the 1851 Religious Census it was found that only nine per cent of people in Wales who attended a place of worship went to Anglican churches while 87 per cent went to **non-conformist** chapels (see below). The census also found that only a third of the population bothered to attend either church or chapel. In 1920 the Prime Minister, Lloyd George, passed through Parliament the Disestablishment of the Church in Wales Act. This set up the Anglican Church of Wales which was independent of the Church of England. Led by the newly appointed Archbishop of Wales, the Welsh church was free to run its own affairs without interference from the Archbishop of Canterbury.

The Chapels also had their critics. The very strict values of the Chapels did turn people away from them. Ministers ... were often opposed to their members attending theatres, sports matches and trade-union meetings, let alone going to the pubs or gambling. Members could be expelled for courting [kissing and cuddling] in public.

SOURCE A

David Egan, *Coal Society* (1987).

Chapel

Ever since the religious revival of the eighteenth century, non-conformist religion has played an important part in Welsh life and culture. As industry and people moved into the South Wales valleys the chapels followed. Religious denominations like the Methodists, Independents and Baptists set up their places of worship in the growing industrial towns and mining villages. In the Rhondda in 1905 there were 151 chapels which could seat nearly 85,000 worshippers – around 80 per cent of the valley's population. These non-conformist groups were popular because they brought religion to the people in an exciting way and in a language they could understand. Sometimes the spirit of enthusiasm caused religious revivals like that of 1904–5 led by Evan Roberts. Roberts, an ex-miner from Loughor, was a preacher of great power and influence. As a result of this revival it has been suggested that by 1907 the numbers attending both church and chapel were higher than they had ever been in Wales.

As well as the very popular Sunday Schools, some chapels went further and established their own day schools or academies. One of the most famous was the Gwynfryn School at Ammanford which was run by Watcyn Williams and John Jenkins between 1880–1914. Having learnt to read the Bible, worshippers could turn to the religious newspapers that were published by the non-conformists. The Baptists had *Seren Gomer*, the Independents had *Y Dysgedydd* and *Y Diwygiwr* and there was the popular quarterly journal *Y Traethodydd*.

SOURCE B

(left) Gellimanwydd chapel in Ammanford c. 1909. During the First World War it was re-named Christian Temple by the Rev. John Davies who was of the opinion that Welsh had no future as a spoken language in the area! He was mistaken.

SOURCE C

(left) Evan Roberts and fellow revivalists from Loughor (c. 1904).

After 1850 the chapels came to see themselves as the guardians of all that was best in Welsh life. Between 1850 and 1900 the chapels developed their choirs, orchestras and even opera and drama groups, their literary and debating societies, their groups for ... social work, their week-night children's ... meetings. By Edwardian times they held [many] *eisteddfodau*, all of which gave Welsh chapel life in this period a sense of humming activity.

SOURCE D

(above) Adapted from Prys Morgan and David Thomas, *Wales: The Shaping of a Nation* (1984).

Religion and Culture

The local and national *eisteddfod* and the local *cymanfa ganu* (singing festivals) were especially popular and they came to be seen as an essential part of Welsh cultural life. In 1905–6 around 285 *cymanfa ganu* festivals were held across Wales with at least 134,000 people taking part. The *eisteddfod* helped keep the language and culture of Wales alive by enabling budding writers, poets, musicians and singers the opportunity to display their talents and compete for prizes. In this way these purely Welsh cultural festivals contributed to the social life and popular entertainment available to the people of Edwardian Wales.

By the early 1920s the chapels were in decline. The bloodshed and suffering caused by the war had turned many against the idea of religion. The more practical issues of politics, work, wages and trade unions became far more important in daily life. As the working classes became better educated they began to question their religion and even criticise some religious ideas and teaching. The world was changing but to many people the chapels and churches seemed slow or incapable of adapting.

?

1 **What do you learn from sources A, B and C about the place of religion in Welsh society?**

2 **a) Why did: (i) the church fail and (ii) the chapels succeed in attracting worshippers?**
   b) What contribution did the chapels make to the cultural life of Wales?

UNIT
4

'Opportunities for all': State Education

The Education Acts of 1870 and 1902

In 1870 the idea of state education was established by an Act of Parliament. The government had realised that the old voluntary system of education was not working very well and that the state would have to provide schools. So England and Wales was divided into 2,500 districts in which locally elected boards of governors had to set up state elementary schools. The idea was such a success that in 1880 the government made schooling for all children under the age of 11 compulsory. It followed this in 1891 by providing these schools free of charge. In 1889 a secondary system of education was introduced into Wales some 13 years before it was introduced into England.

In 1902 Balfour's Education Act abolished the school boards and replaced them with a more efficient system of Local Education Authorities (LEAs) run by local government. These LEAs became responsible for all elementary and technical schools, grammar and secondary schools. But the Liberals disliked the fact that the act also gave money to the voluntary schools run by religious organisations. Because most people in Wales were non-conformist, they resented paying taxes which helped to maintain Catholic and Anglican schools. This led to the so-called 'Welsh Revolt' against the Balfour Act organised by the Liberal MP Lloyd George. As part of this 'revolt' some Liberal councils in Wales refused to enforce the Act. They only did so after their party had won the 1906 election.

The Liberal Education Act of 1906–7

Within a year of winning the 1906 election the Liberals had passed a new Education Act which tried to open up fee-paying grammar schools to all children no matter what their social background or financial situation. All secondary schools which received public money from local rates had to admit up to a quarter of their pupils for free. Elementary school children had to compete for these free places by passing an entrance exam. With these reforms the Liberals hoped to provide all children with a ladder of opportunity.

The Welsh Department of the Board of Education

Thanks largely to the work of Lloyd George, the Liberal government established a new department of education for Wales in 1907. The *South Wales Daily News* welcomed the new department, stating that it had established 'Welsh Home Rule' in education. A distinguished Welsh scholar

Owen M. Edwards was appointed the first Chief Inspector of Schools in Wales. It was hoped that this new department would be more sympathetic to the teaching of Welsh subjects such as Welsh history, literature and the Welsh language.

> *Question*: 'How can Welsh children uphold the Welsh Language?'
> *Answer*: 'By speaking, by reading and by writing it whenever they can – at home or abroad, at work or at play. A good knowledge of Welsh is a thing to be proud of, and all Welsh children should praise their mother tongue accordingly.'

SOURCE A

An extract from a publicity pamphlet issued on St David's Day in 1915 by the Welsh Department of the Board of Education.

The Growth of Literacy

The spread of literacy led to a demand for reading material. Newspapers, magazines and books enjoyed a boom in sales. Newspapers became especially popular because they were cheap, informative and entertaining. In 1910 there were 28 national daily and nine evening newspapers, the most popular being the *Daily Mail*, founded in 1896 and the *Daily Mirror* founded in 1904. The *Mail's* motto was 'explain, simplify and clarify'. A little more expensive and just as popular were the weekly magazines like *Punch*, the *Illustrated London News* and *Lloyd's Weekly News*.

Wales too had its newspapers – both Welsh and English. The most popular in Welsh were the weekly *Baner ac Amserau Cymru* and *Y Genedl Gymreig* to which a young Lloyd George contributed many articles. The only truly Welsh national newspapers were the *South Wales Daily News,* a pro-Liberal publication, and its arch rival the Tory *Western Mail*. The two newspapers fought for a share in the market, a fight lost by the *Daily News* which was forced to close in 1928. There was also a group of local newspapers like the *Cambrian Daily Leader*, the *Rhondda Leader* and the *Merthyr Times* of South Wales and the *Herald Cymraeg* and the *Caernarvon and Denbigh Herald* in the north.

SOURCE B

A contemporary sketch of Lloyd George and the Welsh Liberals' response to Balfour's Education Bill in 1902.

Newspapers gave the better educated working classes the opportunity to widen their horizons and learn about events beyond their own town or village. This caused them to reconsider their attitudes to the world around them.

---

1 a) Sir Arthur Conan Doyle, the creator of Sherlock Holmes, described the elementary schools established by the 1870 Education Act as 'Lighthouses of the future'. Explain what you think he meant by this.
b) How does source B suggest that Lloyd George was more interested in defeating the Conservatives than in helping to promote the education of the children of Wales?

2 How might newspapers have contributed to changing people's attitudes and values between 1906 and 1919? Explain your answer.

UNIT 4

Popular Entertainment

Theatre and Music Halls

Going to the theatre in the West End of London was a social event and one enjoyed by all classes. The well-off paid for the best seats while the rest crowded into the pit and gallery, often having to stand to watch the performances. The most popular form of entertainment in the theatre was the musical comedy; the *Quaker Girl* and *Our Miss Gibbs* were especially favoured by Edwardian audiences. There were also dramatic productions of Shakespeare and plays by George Bernard Shaw.

Music halls were also very popular, particularly with the lower or working classes. For every music hall opened in London some 50 were opening across the country. In 1902 the social reformer Charles Booth reported that 'new halls are opened every year and soon no district will be without one'. Audiences were entertained by such stars as Marie Lloyd and Harry Lauder who were so famous that they could receive fees of £1,000 a week. However, the people of places like Cardiff and Swansea or Bradford and Manchester would not have had the pleasure of being entertained by the great stars of the period. They had to make do with lesser talents and touring companies.

SOURCE A

The opening of the Empire Music Hall, Tonypandy, in 1909.

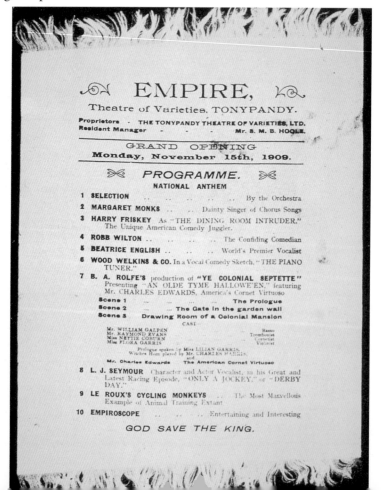

The Cinema

The first film feature (or silent moving picture as it was called) had appeared in 1895. It was an instant hit with audiences. Soon film-makers were touring towns and villages to show off their features in makeshift tents. By 1900 music halls were beginning to show these features as part of their entertainment and in time cinema halls appeared like the Carlton in Swansea in 1914. The Carlton was the first purpose-built cinema in Wales. According to one eyewitness, 'these pictures have made an extraordinary difference to the leisure hours of the working class ... to whom they seem to give untiring delight'. During the war the most popular entertainer on film was British-born Charlie Chaplin. His American-made comedies were said to have established the cinema as the 'poor man's theatre'.

SOURCE B

A cinema audience enjoy the Keystone Cops in the film *Made for Laughs* in 1913.

Sport

Two of the most popular sports in Wales were rugby and soccer. Although it was an English game imported to Wales, rugby became the sport of the working man of the South Wales valleys. As early as 1881 the representatives of the rugby clubs of Swansea, Cardiff, Llanelli, Newport, Lampeter, Llandeilo, Brecon, Llandovery, Merthyr, Pontypool and Bangor met to establish the Welsh Rugby Union. Soon matches were being organised between the countries of the United Kingdom and in 1893 Wales won its first Triple Crown. The match that caught the public's imagination was Wales against the New Zealand All Blacks in 1905. The All Blacks were unbeaten in 27 games of their tour of the British Isles, which included matches against England, Scotland and Ireland. It was thought that their match against Wales would be won easily. However, in a thrilling encounter watched by a crowd of 45,000, Wales won. The sport of rugby became ever more popular as a result.

The Welsh were less successful at soccer. They managed to beat England only twice between 1879 and 1919. But despite their lack of international success the sport grew at local level and several clubs were established which were able to compete in the English league. Magazines and picture comics were published which popularised the game, especially among the young. The era of mass entertainment had arrived.

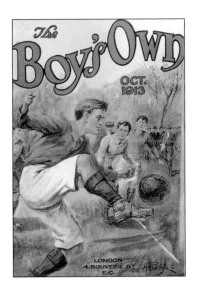

SOURCE C

The cover of the *Boy's Own* magazine (1913).

1 a) Read source A. What type of entertainment was available to the people of Tonypandy?

2 What effect might: (i) the cinema and (ii) sport have had on the daily life of the people of Wales?

3 How might the spread of 'popular' entertainment have contributed to decline in Welsh language and culture?

OVERVIEW

Consider the following key question. How and why did people's attitudes and values change in the period 1906–19?

Depression, War
AND
Recovery
1930–1951

UNIT 1: LIFE IN THE DEPRESSION

Key Issue: *In what ways and to what extent did changes in the economic fortunes of Wales and England affect people's lives in the 1930s?*

'Decline of the old, growth of the new':
Industrial and Economic Change 84

Focus: The General Strike, 1926 88

Unemployment, Poverty and the Means Test . .90

Focus: Wales and the Depression I:
Hardship and Despair? .92

Focus: Wales and the Depression II:
Popular Protests 95

Wales and England in the 1930s:
Contrasts and Connections 98

Immigration and Emigration:
The Welsh Experience 100

Sport and Popular Entertainment 102

Wales in Books; Wales on Film 106

UNIT 2: BRITAIN AND THE THREAT OF GERMANY

Key Issue: *Why did Britain go to war with Germany in 1939?*

Democracy or Dictatorship?
The Changing Face of Europe 108

British Foreign Policy between the Wars:
Appeasement 110

Neville Chamberlain, Munich and
the Drift to War 114

Focus: The Reactions of the British Press to
Hitler and Appeasement 118

Fascism and the British People 120

Focus: Penyberth and Welsh Nationalism 122

UNIT 3: WAR ON THE HOME FRONT

Key Issue: *How did people in Wales and England cope with the experiences of the Second World War?*

Britain Goes to War, 1939 126

The Second World War in Europe, 1939–45 . . .128

The Blitz 130

Focus: Swansea and the Three Nights' Blitz . . .132

Life in Wartime Britain 134

Profile: Winston Churchill 140

UNIT 4: POST-WAR WALES AND ENGLAND

Key Issue: *How and to what extent did the economic and social policies of the Labour governments change Wales and England in the period 1945–51?*

The End of War, the End of Empire:
Britain in 1945 142

'A different Britain':
The 1945 General Election 144

Post-war Reconstruction and
the Labour Government 146

'From the cradle to the grave':
Establishing the Welfare State 148

Focus: The National Health Service 152

Profile: Anuerin Bevan 154

Nationalisation 156

'Set the people free': The Defeat of Labour . . .158

1930	Unemployment rises in South Wales. Beginning of mass emigration from Wales.
1931	Economic and political crises. MacDonald leads a coalition government. One-time Conservative MP and former Labour Cabinet Minister, Sir Oswald Mosley, forms a new political party of fascists.
1932	World Disarmament Conference begins.
1933	Unemployment figures, factory and mine closures reach their peak in South Wales. Hitler comes to power in Germany.
1934	World Disarmament Conference ends without agreement.
1935	Stanley Baldwin becomes Prime Minister of a Conservative government. Stay-down strikes at many collieries in South Wales. King George V dies. Succeeded by Edward VIII. Italy invades Abyssinia.
1936	Abdication crisis. Edward VIII abdicates. Succeeded by George VI. Peace Pledge Union founded – Britain's largest pacifist organisation. German troops re-occupy the Rhineland. RAF bombing school at Penyberth burned down by Welsh Nationalists. Lloyd George meets with Hitler in Germany. Outbreak of the Spanish Civil War. Large numbers of Welshmen join the International Brigade to fight in Spain. Jarrow Crusade against unemployment.
1937	Neville Chamberlain becomes Prime Minister.
1938	Germany unites with Austria. Czechoslovakian crisis. The Four Powers meet in Munich.
1939	Germany occupies the whole of Czechoslovakia. The first Welsh language primary school opens. Germany invades Poland. Britain and France declare war on Germany. Outbreak of the Second World War.

1940	Chamberlain resigns as Prime Minister. Succeeded by Winston Churchill. Fall of France.
1941	Japanese bomb Pearl Harbor in Hawaii. Germany invades Russia. The USA and the USSR enter the war. Aneurin Bevan attacks Winston Churchill's conduct of the war in the House of Commons. Churchill wins vote of confidence in Parliament.
1942	German army defeated by the British at the Battle of El Alamein in Egypt, North Africa. British and American troops invade Morocco and Algeria, North Africa.
1943	Germans defeated by the Russians at the Battle of Stalingrad. German and Italian armies surrender in North Africa. Allies invade Italy.
1944	Education Act passed. D-Day landings. Allies invade France.
1945	The Second World War ends in the defeat of Germany. Labour has a landslide victory in the general election. Clement Attlee replaces Churchill as Prime Minister. Lloyd George dies.
1946	Labour nationalises the Bank of England. National Health Service Act passed.
1947	Coal industry nationalised. India given independence.
1948	National Health Service set up by Anuerin Bevan.
1950	Labour narrowly wins the general election. Outbreak of the Korean War. British troops sent to fight alongside other United Nations forces.
1951	Labour loses the general election. Churchill succeeds Attlee as Prime Minister.

UNIT 1

LIFE IN THE DEPRESSION

'Decline of the old, growth of the new': Industrial and Economic Change

> **KEY ISSUE:**
> *In what ways and to what extent did changes in the economic fortunes of Wales and England affect people's lives in the 1930s?*

According to the historian Bryn O' Callaghan, 'There were really two Britains in the 1920s and 1930s. There was the Britain which depended for its living on the old, staple industries such as coal and shipbuilding. The other Britain was built on new industries making new products – motor vehicles, electrical goods, man-made fibres'. Wales and the Welsh people belonged to that half of Britain still dependent on the heavy industries of coal, steel, iron, tinplate and slate.

Old Industries

SOURCE A

An industrial map of Britain, c.1930.

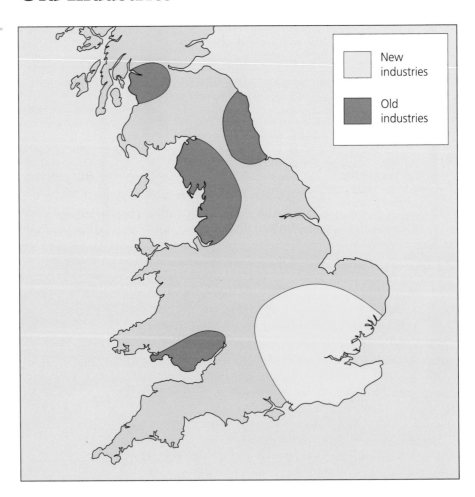

	New industries
	Old industries

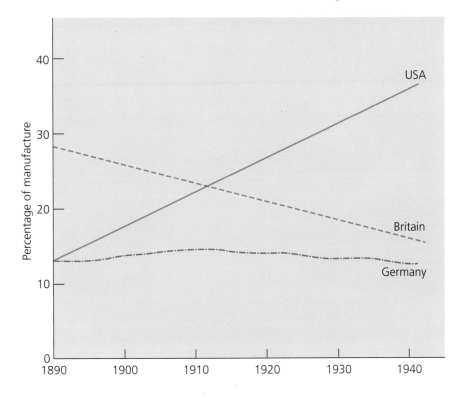

A graph showing the percentage share of the manufacturing world export market of Britain, the USA and Germany.

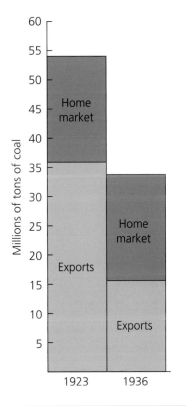

SOURCE C

British coal production in 1923 and 1936.

Before the Great War Britain's prosperity had depended on the sale of heavy industrial goods like coal and steel. However, at the end of the war these older industries entered a period of decline. Rising costs and a failure to invest in new technology and machinery caused problems. There was a fall in demand for British goods and increased competition from abroad, particularly from the USA and Germany. The more expensive British goods could not compete with cheaper imports. To make matters worse, Britain's traditional pre-war export market – countries like Australia, Canada and New Zealand – were no longer prepared to 'buy British'. They bought American steel, German coal, Japanese ships and Indian cotton instead. This brought to an end the so-called 'golden age' of Welsh and British heavy industry.

The decline in the older industries caused unemployment to rise. About 800,000 jobs were lost due to the fall in overseas exports alone. The decline in the cotton industry of Lancashire and the north west of England provides a good example of how badly hit these industries were by the pace of change and competition. Cotton had been Britain's most important pre-war export. Between 1909 and 1911 Britain had enjoyed a 65 per cent share in the world cotton market but by 1938 this had fallen to 28 per cent. The number of people employed in the industry fell from 621,500 in 1911 to 393,000 in 1938.

Wales had no cotton mills but it had coal mines. In 1913, 485 collieries, employing over 250,000 miners, produced 57 million tons of coal. More than half of this total was exported. For three years after 1918 the coal industry enjoyed a boom. More coal than ever before was being mined and exported from the ports of Cardiff, Barry, Penarth and Swansea. However, investment in modern technology meant that French, German and Polish mines were producing more coal and at a cheaper price than could be mined in Wales.

SOURCE D

A contemporary photograph showing the mass production of biscuits.

New Industries

As the traditional heavy industries declined, the new light industries began to take their place. These industries tended to concentrate on consumer goods such as cars, cookers, fridges and radios. The goods were mass produced for an expanding market in modern factories equipped with the latest technology. Advertising encouraged consumers to buy the new cars, motorbikes, radios and household gadgets on the hire purchase system. This new system of credit meant that even the most expensive items could be bought by the ordinary consumer.

When mass production methods were applied to the motor car industry the number of cars sold in Britain rose from 132,000 in 1913 to about 2 million in 1938. In 1923 the most popular car on the market was the Austin Seven which sold for £225. But, by 1936, cheaper production costs meant the price had fallen to £125.

The technology and machinery used in the growing light industries used a relatively new source of power – electricity. Electricity was clean, cheap and efficient and it began to replace coal as the nation's main fuel supply. In 1926 the Central Electricity Board was set up to supply the needs of industry, but British homes were also given the opportunity to go 'on the mains'. Between 1920 and 1938 the number of consumers supplied with electricity increased from 730,000 to 9 million.

The government encouraged these new industries by offering grants and by setting up industrial estates. It was thought that those made unemployed by the old industries would find jobs in the new industries. This did not happen although over 400,000 people left South Wales between 1920 and 1939 for work in other parts of Britain, mainly in London, the Midlands and the south east of England. Far too many people were being made redundant for the new consumer industries to take them all. Also, the new skills needed to work in the consumer industries required re-training, a costly exercise for which the government was unwilling to pay. With the exception of the aircraft and chemical industries, the factories of these light industries were much smaller and they employed 1 million fewer people. By the late 1930s the sale of British consumer goods still only accounted for 15 per cent of the nation's total exports.

zip fasteners	radios
cameras	rayon materials (man made fibres)
motor cars	electric irons
light bulbs	cookers
vacuum cleaners	ballpoint pens
fridges	toothpaste
potato crisps	bakelite (plastic)
hair dryers	

SOURCE E

A list of the goods mass produced by the new industries in the 1930s.

SOURCE F

This advert for the new electric vacuum cleaner appeared on screen at the cinema in 1938.

1 a) What is meant by the phrase 'heavy or staple industries'?
b) Why did they decline during the first half of the century?
c) By how much did British coal production drop between 1923 and 1936?

2 a) Using sources D, E and F to help you, why did the demand for electricity increase during the 1920s and 30s.
b) What impact would the list of goods in source E have had on the 'ordinary individual'?

The General Strike, 1926

> Next May we shall be faced with the greatest crisis and the greatest struggle we have ever known and we are preparing for it.

SOURCE A

(above) An extract from a speech made by A.J. Cook, the leader of the South Wales Miners, August 1925.

In 1925 competition from abroad led to a fall in the demand for British coal. This convinced mine owners that a reduction in wages was urgently needed. The miners were determined to fight any cuts so they asked the Trades Union Congress (TUC) to support them in a strike if these cuts went ahead. The Prime Minister Stanley Baldwin tried to avoid a confrontation by setting up a Commission headed by Sir Herbert Samuel to investigate the issue. In March 1926 the Samuel Commission advised Baldwin that a cut in wages and a longer working day was necessary. The mining union failed to reach an agreement with the mine owners and on 1 May 1926 the owners announced the closure of the mines. The miners were 'locked out'. Talks between the TUC and the government failed to solve the dispute and on 3 May a General Strike was called. It lasted nine days. But the miners refused to go back to work and remained on strike for a further seven months before finally giving in.

How did the Strike begin?

SOURCE B

(right) An extract from the diary of the Labour Party Leader, Ramsey MacDonald, 2 May 1926.

It really looks as though there is to be a General Strike to save Mr Cook's face ... The election of this fool as miners' secretary looks as though it will be the most calamitous [disastrous] thing that ever happened to the trade union movement. The chief criminal, however, is the Government.

SOURCE C

(right) An extract from a letter written by the TUC to Stanley Baldwin, 3 May 1926.

The Trade Union representatives were astounded [shocked] to learn that ... negotiations had been abruptly terminated [ended] by the Government ... The public will judge the nature of the Government's intentions ... the sincere [honest] work ... to obtain an honourable settlement has been wrecked.

SOURCE D

(right) An extract from the *Daily Herald*, 4 May 1926.

The miners are locked out to enforce reductions of wages and an increase in hours. The Government stands behind the mineowners. It had rebuffed [ignored] the Trade Union Movement's every effort to ... [find] ... an honourable peace ... The Unions are fighting to maintain the standard of life of the great mass of the people.

SOURCE E

(right) An extract from the *Daily Mail,* 4 May 1926.

A general strike is not an industrial dispute. It is a revolutionary movement intended to inflict suffering ... and thereby to put force ... upon the Government.

Strikers and the Authorities

At Maerdy, where the Communist Party is stronger than in any other place in the Rhondda, the Ferndale police raided the house of two well known Maerdy men. News of the raid spread through the town and a crowd of many hundreds gathered. The police were only 5 in number and the crowd made a hostile demonstration marked by much booing and singing of the 'Red Flag'.

SOURCE F

(left) An extract from the *Western Mail*, 7 May 1926.

UNDER WHICH FLAG?

JOHN BULL. "ONE OF THESE TWO FLAGS HAS GOT TO COME DOWN—AND IT WON'T BE MINE."

Pontypool magistrates sentence a newsagent, Frederick Charles Chapman, to 1 month hard labour for putting the following questions and answers on a poster in his shop window:

Child: What is a blackleg, Daddy?

Father: A blackleg is a traitor my boy, who knows not honour or shame.

Child: Are there any in the Eastern Valley, Daddy?

Father: No, my boy, only the station master at Abersychan and two clerks at Crane Street Station.

Child: I am glad you are not a blackleg, Daddy.

SOURCE G

(above) An extract from the *Western Mail*, 24 May 1926.

SOURCE H

(above) This cartoon first appeared in *Punch* but was reprinted by government order on the front page of *The British Gazette*, 12 May 1926.

The End of the Strike

... in the decisive defeat of the miners in the 1926 General Strike. No strike pay was available, and everyone had to rally round to raise money. Soup kitchens were set up in local church halls, co-operative boot centres were set up and farmers were persuaded to donate meat, fruit and vegetables. Groups of miners regularly travelled to neighbouring English counties to sing and beg for money...

SOURCE I

(left) An extract from HTV's: *Guide to Welsh History* (1989).

1 a) Which of the newspapers were: (i) for and (ii) against the miners and the TUC? Give reasons for your answers.
b) According to sources F, G and I, what were some of the effects of the strike on the people of the South Wales valleys?

2 a) Below are some of the reasons which help explain why the strike failed. Match the sources to the reasons. Use the list as a plan for your essay in question 2 (b).
● The government refused to discuss an end to the strike.

● The government used the radio and newspapers to spread propaganda against the strikers.
● The Labour Party was divided in its support for the miners.
● People feared that the unions were trying to overthrow the government and set up a soviet-style communist regime.
● The mining unions did not have enough money to support the strike for long.
● The government used the law to frighten supporters of the miners.
b) Write an essay explaining why the General Strike failed.

UNIT **1**

<small>LIFE IN THE DEPRESSION</small>

Unemployment, Poverty and the Means Test

The collapse of the post-war economic boom in 1921, increased competition from abroad, the disaster of the General Strike of 1926 and the decline in the mining and steel industries crippled the Welsh economy. Wales was already suffering from the effects of depression when in 1929 matters took a turn for the worse.

The Great Depression

A massive financial crisis in the USA, known as the Wall Street Crash, led to the collapse of the largest, richest and most powerful economy in the world. Britain, Europe and many of the world's industrial powers had come to depend on American loans and trade so that when its economy crashed so did theirs. This was the beginning of the Great Depression.

UNEMPLOYMENT

One of the main effects of the depression was the massive rise in unemployment and poverty. By 1933 world unemployment topped 30 million people, of whom some 3 million were British, around 13 million were American and 6 million were German. The worst hit areas in Britain were those still dependent on the old heavy industries. By 1938 the unemployment rate in each of the four basic heavy industries of coal, cotton, shipbuilding and iron and steel, was twice what it was in other forms of employment. In these areas unemployment became a way of life.

According to the post-war Census returns of 1921 around 54 per cent of the male population of Wales were employed in or dependent upon some industry or other. Out of this total, 47 per cent worked in the coalmining industry followed by nearly 14 per cent in iron and steel-making. Another

SOURCE A

The total number of people registered as unemployed in Glamorganshire, Wales and Britain (1928–38). (Adapted from H. P. Fogarty, *Prospects of the Industrial Areas of Great Britain,* (1945).

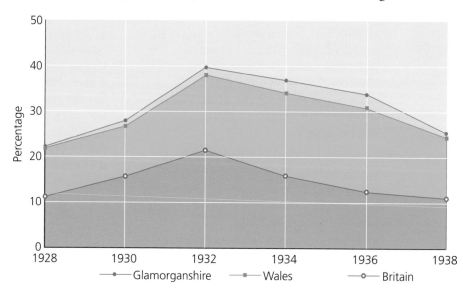

17 per cent worked in transport such as railways and haulage. With such a high percentage of the working population dependent on the declining heavy industries, Wales was bound to suffer in the depression.

GOVERNMENT RESPONSE

In 1931 a National Government was set up, led by Labour's Ramsay MacDonald. This coalition government of mainly Conservatives with some Labour and Liberal MPs tried to cope with the worsening crisis. Unfortunately, they had few ideas. Some politicians like Labour's Sir Oswald Mosley called for massive government spending to create jobs and high tariffs on foreign imports to protect British industry. Others thought that the economy would sort itself out and that politicians should not interfere – in the long run all would be well. Many more had no idea how to solve the crisis. Lloyd George, leader of the opposition Liberals, tried to persuade the government to accept Mosley's plan for action.
They rejected it.

THE MEANS TEST

The government responded to the crisis by trying to cut costs. The first target of these cuts were the benefits paid to the unemployed. A man without work could claim benefit under the unemployment insurance scheme. This was known as the dole and it was paid for the first six months of unemployment. The usual rate was 15s. (75p) per week for man and wife and about 5s. (25p) for each child. In 1931 the dole was cut by 10 per cent and **means tested** for the first time. An unemployed man now had to prove he needed the dole.

However, as unemployment continued to rise the government was faced by a new problem. What should it do about those people who had been unemployed for more than six months and had used up their dole? As the cost of benefits rose there were calls to reduce them further. In an effort to avoid bad publicity the government passed the Unemployment Act of 1934 which set up the Unemployment Assistance Boards (UABs). The UABs were responsible for managing the Means Test and ensuring that benefits were paid only to those who were 'desperately in need' and then only if they were 'actively seeking work'.

SOURCE B

Election posters issued by the National Government.

1 **What were the characteristic features of the Great Depression in Britain?**

2 **a) How did Parliament acknowledge the seriousness of the economic crisis?**
b) What do the dole, Means Test and UABs show about the attitude of the government towards the: (i) economic depression and (ii) unemployed?

3 **Study source B.**
a) What is the message of the posters?
b) Who were they aimed at?
c) How successful do you think they might have been?

Wales and the Depression I: Hardship and Despair?

The depression hit Wales as hard, if not harder, than most of the other parts of Britain. In 1932 the Ministry of Labour published the unemployment figures for Wales. It stood at an all time high of 258,000 or 28.5 per cent of the working population. In the Rhondda valley, in 1934, 61 per cent of the population were registered as unemployed while in Merthyr Tydfil the figure stood at 69 per cent.

Of course, statistics can only hint at the hardship and despair suffered by these people. The country was not only depressed – it was a depressing place to be. One famous Welsh writer and poet, Dylan Thomas (1914–53), was glad to leave his native Swansea for the bright lights of London.

Mrs E.M. W ... of Pontypool.
There are nine in the family, the ages of the children being 14, 13, 11, 7, 5, 3 and 2. The income from all sources is £2 7s. [£2.35] a week. ... all food has to be cooked on the open fire ... the family has only one kettle, one small frying pan, two small saucepans. [Dishes] for preparing food consist of only one bowl, which is used for making puddings and to wash up in. They have only seven cups and saucers between nine ... two knives, six small spoons, six forks, and eight plates.

The family live in three rooms, one living-kitchen and two small bedrooms. The bedclothing is very threadbare [worn] and has little warmth. The small bed does not belong to them; they have it only on loan. The house is old and very damp and cold.

In a statement [written by a witness] ... he says: 'I have known the family for a number of years. Both parents are very sober and industrious persons and the mother strives [works] very hard to keep her children clean and respectable. The family endeavoured [tried] to get a special grant from the UAB in order that they could make good the [lack of] household goods, but this was refused. The mother is now suffering from a skin disease which is considered to have been brought on by poor quality food and nervous tension.'

SOURCE A

An extract from *The Problem of the Distressed Areas*, a survey of unemployment and poverty in Wales by Wal Harrington (1937).

It wasn't all sad. We had loads of laughs. Everyone was in the same boat. There was always someone whistling or singing. We had no wireless [radio], but there was always life. A lot of people in the street went on holiday, camping or to Barry Island.

No members of the family were employed at this time. There was no employment about at that time. Jobs were so few and far between that people used to look in the *Echo* [a newspaper] and if they found that someone had died, they'd be round the place of work trying to get the job before the burial!

We always had plenty of food. We were never short of it. We never bought 'scraps'. There was plenty of food in the shops if you had the money to buy it. We were the only people in the street to drink fresh milk.

SOURCE B

Mrs Catherine Reason of Cardiff (b. 1902) quoted in *The Experiences of Wales in the Depression* (1986).

Keen as the resentment is throughout the valleys ... against the new part II regulations [Means Test], the procession had the atmosphere of a Gymanfa Ganu [singing festival] or a Sunday School rally. There were smiles, jokes and laughter on every side. Men wore good-looking overcoats and suits, young fellows, many of them unemployed, wore smartly cut clothes, looking the mirror of fashion; young women walked in attractive hats, smart coats and dainty high heeled shoes. There was little outward indication of poverty ... such as ... the unemployed are experiencing now.

A true blue Tory supporter of the National Government would undoubtedly have pointed an accusing finger ... and said, 'Bah! where is your poverty and hardship?

SOURCE C

An extract from a local Welsh newspaper, the *Aberdare Leader*, describing a protest demonstration (1935).

The district has again had a continued epidemic of scarlet fever during the year ... and the severity of the symptoms were, in my opinion, due to general malnutrition among the children, the result of the unfortunate economic conditions ... in South Wales.

SOURCE D

An extract from a report by Dr Rankin, Chief Medical Officer for Gelligaer District Council (1933).

SOURCE E

'Work at last'. A cartoon from the *Daily Express* (1936). The artist shows the military 'shape' of possible work for the future.

SOURCE F

A contemporary photograph of an unemployed man seeking work in the 1930s.

? 1 a) Explain what: (i) industrious and (ii) UAB mean in source A.
b) Why was the full name of the person referred to in source A not given?
c) What does this tell us about the effects of the depression on some peoples' lives?
d) Give reasons for the differences in the women's experiences of the depression as presented in sources A and B.

2 a) Read source C. If the people who protested were so poor, how could they be as well dressed as described here?
b) With so much unemployment, poverty and illness (source D) in these 'distressed areas', how do you account for the good humour of the protest demonstration?

Wales and the Depression II: Popular Protests

In 1936 King Edward VIII toured Wales to see for himself the hardship and poverty caused by the depression. He was visibly upset by what he saw and shocked by the stories he was told by the unemployed people he met. He was reported to have said, 'Something must be done'. His visit was welcomed by most people of South Wales because of the publicity it brought. They knew that he would be followed by large numbers of journalists and cameramen from home and abroad. It was hoped that the government might take more notice of their desperate situation and do something about it. But nothing was done.

Within months of his visit to Wales the King had **abdicated**. The poor and hungry of the South Wales valleys were forgotten as the nation and the world turned their attention to the royal crisis. This convinced many people that there was no alternative but to protest. A mass demonstration with popular support and maximum publicity might force the government into positive action. 'Hunger marches', like those which had taken place in previous years, were organised and thousands of people became involved in protesting against the continuing unemployment and hardship.

> Today you will be visiting the towns and villages of our valleys ... We regret that your tour has been planned in such a way that the terrible effects of this poverty will not be seen.

SOURCE A

(above) A letter addressed to King Edward VIII from some people in Pontypool published in the *Western Mail*, November 1936.

South Wales Marchers' Organising Council.

SOUTH WALES MINERS'
MARCH TO LONDON

CALL TO ACTION!   VOLUNTEERS WANTED!

Arising out of the pronouncement by A. J. COOK, 18/9/27, a Miners' March to London from S. Wales is being organised. The March will commence on the day Parliament opens--Nov. 8th, and the Marchers will arrive in London on Nov. 20th, where they will be received by an <u>All London</u> Working Class Demonstration.

The object of the March shall be two-fold, to arouse a Nation-wide feeling concerning the Appalling Conditions in the Mine-fields created by the policy of the Government and the Coal-owners, and to seek an interview with the Prime Minister, the Minister of Mines, the Minister of Labour, and the Minister of Health.

The purpose of such interview shall be:

1. To draw attention to the Chronic Destitution affecting Unemployed and Employed Miners arising out of the Failure of Private Enterprise in the Mining Industry.
2. To draw the attention of the Government to the persistent Closing of Mines, thus causing further widespread Unemployment.
3. To point out the consequences of the 8-hour Day.
4. To urge the Government to make Satisfactory Provision for the Employment of those Unemployed.
5. To demand State Aid to permit Guardians to more effectively Relieve Distress.
6. To protest against the Continuous Disqualification of Men and Women from Benefit at the Labour Exchange, and to urge More Adequate Scales of Benefit.
7. To press for a system of Adequate Pensioning of Miners over Sixty Years of age as a means of Reducing the Number of Unemployed.

☞ Those wishing to Enrol as Recruits for this Historic March should make application at once to:

THE TRAGEDY OF THE MINEFIELDS MUST BE MADE KNOWN!

SOURCE B

(left) A contemporary poster publicising the 1927 hunger march to London.

SOURCE C

(right) A hunger march to Bristol in 1931.

We hear a little too much about depressed Wales, and not quite enough of what the ... spirit of Wales [has] achieved in bringing about her own recovery.

SOURCE D

(above) An extract from a speech by Sir Thomas Inskip, Minister of Defence, as reported in *The Times* (1936).

SOURCE E

(right) An extract from a letter written by W.H. Mainwaring M.P. to a government minister (1935).

The Minister, perhaps, can ... imagine the depth of feeling [in the Rhondda] when I tell him that... there is a total population of less than 140,000 and a week ago yesterday, 100,000 people demonstrated there. There was nobody in that district who was not demonstrating except those who were in hospital. I only wish to God that the same thing [would happen] in London.

SOURCE F

(right) A report in the *Daily Worker* newspaper (1932).

Not the slightest mention on any of the film newsreels of the Hunger Marches or of the tremendous London demonstrations. I have been looking out for them in the London cinemas but cannot find a trace; I suppose the same is true of all the provincial [local] cinemas ...

It would be interesting to discover whether this suppression [keeping from the public] of a vitally important newsreel item was due to the action of the film companies themselves, or to intervention by the censor or ... by the government.

At any rate ... the Hunger Marches and the demonstrations and the [police] baton charges are not news; but the visit of Princess Ingrid ... is very important news, as also is the visit of the Arsenal football team to France, and a woman swinging by her teeth over New York ... and so on.

Once I was living in Wales and could see much more clearly the ... humiliating and devastating [terrible] effect of unemployment on people particularly in the valleys, where all hope seemed to be gone. Men were standing on the street corners ... not knowing what to do with themselves – people [were] really hungry. Well you couldn't not take part in any activity which would make people themselves feel that at least they were fighting back and also you felt it was absolutely essential to get other people to understand the enormity [great seriousness] of the situation.

SOURCE G

(left) An interview in 1985 with Mrs Dora Cox, who took part in the hunger march of 1934.

People who have lived in the valley all their lives were sure that they had never witnessed such a scene of protest ... It was not a movement initiated [begun] by any particular party, but a united front of [Union] Officials, Communists, Ministers of Religion and business and professional men, with members of Parliament, Magistrates and Councillors, rubbing shoulders with all sections of the populace [people].

SOURCE H

(left) An extract from a report in the *Rhondda Leader*, a local newspaper (1935).

SOURCE I

(left) Police drafted in to Blaengarw to deter protest marches.

So many remedies [solutions] have been tried in vain. South Wales has become a bore. It is like a crying babe in the hands of an ignorant mother. It is smacked by one [government] department and kissed by another. Why won't it go to sleep like Dorsetshire?

SOURCE J

(left) A pamphlet entitled 'What's Wrong with Wales' issued by The *New Statesman and Nation magazine* (1935).

1 a) **What effect might the information in sources D, I and J have had on the people of South Wales?**
b) **What do sources D, E, F and I reveal about the attitude of the government towards the unemployed of South Wales after more than six years of depression?**
c) **With the help and support of the government the King visited South** Wales to see for himself the poverty and hardship in the valleys. In view of this, how do you account for the letter in the *Western Mail* (source A)?

2 a) **Using the sources and other information on pages 88–89 and 92–94, why did people protest?**
b) **Judging from the information in source E, how successful would you regard the hunger marches?**

LIFE IN THE DEPRESSION

Wales and England in the 1930s: Contrasts and Connections

The prosperous south east of England was a world away from the depressed south east of Wales. New investment, new housing, better roads and efficient rail transport transformed London and the surrounding areas. Businessmen and industrialists found it cheaper and easier to set up a factory in somewhere like Slough than in a place like Merthyr Tydfil. London and the densely populated south east could provide a skilled workforce and a ready market for buying the goods. Eighty per cent of the new factories built and 65 per cent of the new jobs created between 1931 and 1937 were in London and south-east England. There was little outward sign of poverty in these areas.

SOURCE A

(right) Kenneth Morgan, *Rebirth of a Nation: Wales 1880–1980* (1981).

Some historians ... have [recently] tended to paint a more cheerful picture of the thirties ... No doubt, amongst the owner-occupiers [home owners] of London, the home counties, and the east Midlands, with their cars, their housing estates, their thriving new light industries based on consumer durables [goods] ... the thirties were not such a bad time in which to live. But in South Wales ... a whole society was crucified [devastated] by mass unemployment and near-starvation.

The north of England had more in common with South Wales than with southern England. Both regions suffered high unemployment and economic decline. When the government did nothing to prevent the shipyards from closing in the north east of England, 75 per cent of Jarrow's workers became unemployed. In an effort to meet the Prime Minister, 200 of them marched 300 miles to London. Newsreel cameramen and press photographers marched with them and recorded every day of the 14-day trek south. Along the route the marchers were blessed in a service in Ripon Cathedral, they were joined by politicians such as Helen Wilkinson, the Labour MP for Jarrow, and they had their boots mended free of charge by the Leicester Co-op. They marched to the sound of mouth organs and they were fed and sheltered by sympathisers along the way.

This was perhaps the most famous protest march of the 1930s but it achieved little. Unfortunately for the shipbuilders of Jarrow and the coalminers of the Rhondda, the power to cure unemployment lay with the politicians who sat in Parliament in the wealthy London borough of Westminster. In an effort to attract industry and jobs to Tyneside and Wales, the government passed the Special Areas Act in 1934. As a result of this Act government grants were made available to tempt industrialists to these areas. But government critics said that this Act was too little and too late.

SOURCE B

(above) The Jarrow Marchers on their way to London in 1936.

% unemployed in England and Wales, 1934

Place	%
Jarrow	67.8
Merthyr Tydfil	61.9
Mountain Ash	56.7
Abertillery	49.6
Sunderland	36.3
London	8.6
Birmingham	6.4
Oxford	5.1
St. Albans	3.9

	No of workers per thousand unemployed for a year or more, summer 1936
Coal miners	123
Shipbuilders and repairers	95
Cotton workers	67
Builders and building labourers	24
Furniture workers	21
Workers in motor vehicles, cycles etc.	10

SOURCE C

(below and left) Prosperity and poverty in Britain: some facts and figures (adapted from various sources).

Place	Death of babies per thousand live births in 1935
Jarrow	114
Sunderland	92
Scotland	77
Home counties	42

SOURCE D

(left) The contrasting halves of Britain: (i) Dagenham in Essex and (ii) Jarrow on Tyneside (1931).

The contrast between poverty and prosperity was clear within Wales itself. There might have been a housing shortage in Pontypridd or slum housing in Merthyr during the thirties but in the Uplands in Swansea, Garden Village in Wrexham and Cyncoed and Roath in Cardiff hundreds of private houses were built for a prosperous middle class. Unemployment in the Rhondda and Rhymney valleys was nearly four times that of Cardiff. However, some new industries like the chemical industry opened plants on Tyneside in the north east of England and in North Wales. As a result of grants under the Special Areas Act, the steel industry built a new plant in Ebbw Vale and a new road running along the Heads of the Valleys was constructed, both of which created hundreds of jobs.

1 **a) In what ways does source C support the belief that the south east of England was little affected by the depression?**
b) How do the infant mortality rates of 1935 add to our knowledge of the effects of the depression?
c) What were: (i) the similarities between South Wales and the north **of England, and (ii) the differences between the south east of England and South Wales?**
The information on pages 84–87 may help here.

2 *Interpretation of history.*
What does the information in source A tell us about the way the 1930s have been interpreted?

LIFE IN THE DEPRESSION

Immigration and Emigration: The Welsh Experience

For much of the nineteenth century and up until the beginning of the Great War in 1914 Wales had attracted thousands of immigrants. They came from various parts of the United Kingdom in search of work in the coal mines and steel plants of the south east and north east of Wales. Most of the immigrants who settled in the Rhondda valley came from the west of England. Further west in the coalfields of the Amman valley they came largely from within Wales itself and from the West Midlands and Lancashire. Many Irish people settled in Merthyr, the Cynon valley, Swansea, Cardiff, Newport and Port Talbot. However, the post-war depression of the 1920s and the Great Depression of the 1930s reduced the flow of immigrants to a trickle. Within a few short years pre-war immigration into Wales had turned into post-war emigration from Wales on a massive scale. Close to 440,000 people left Wales between 1921 and 1939 in search of work and a better life.

SOURCE A

Deian Hopkin, 'Social Reactions to Economic Change' in *Wales between the Wars* (1988).

[An] indication of demographic [population] change is revealed by the statistics for the Welsh language ... It was the decline in Welsh speakers as a whole that was most serious ... Much of the decline arose because a substantial sector of the population was fleeing.

Census records showing the total number of Welsh speakers in Wales.

1911 – 977,366	
1921 – 922,092	
1931 – 909,261	
1951 – 714,686	

Emigration Abroad

During the 1920s a large number of Welsh people left Britain altogether. For many of them the United States was seen as a land of opportunity. It had bright, glittering cities like New York, Los Angeles and San Francisco, but more importantly it had work. In one American town a large number of ex-Tredegar people successfully established their own Welsh community. Still more Welsh émigrés sought work in Australia, Canada and New Zealand. However, with the Great Depression of 1929 emigration abroad virtually came to an end.

Migration to England

For those who did not wish to leave the United Kingdom the only alternative was to seek work in the wealthier regions of England. Thousands of Welsh workers and their families were encouraged to leave

Wales by the government. The Ministry of Labour set up a scheme to help unemployed workers willing to move to popular areas like London, Coventry, Watford, Slough and Oxford. There they were employed in light engineering and car manufacturing. One of the biggest employers of Welsh workers was the Morris motor car company at Cowley in Oxford.

The migration of so many people from Wales to England had serious consequences for some parts of the country. The population of the Rhondda fell by 13 per cent in the 1920s and possibly by as much as 18 per cent in the 1930s so that by 1951 there were around 111,000 compared to the 162,000 of 20 years earlier. Merthyr Tydfil also suffered a sharp decline in its population. About 26,600 people left the town between 1921 and 1939.

SOURCE B

In 1936 a survey was made of the effects of migration on the churches in the Rhondda valley. It was found that 8,867 members of the Nonconformist chapels of the Rhondda had moved away between 1925 and 1935 ... the total loss of members due to migration cannot be less than 10,000.

Brinley Thomas, 'The changing face of South Wales' in the *Listener* magazine (1938).

SOURCE C

Estimated loss of population by migration calculated from the Census returns 1931 to mid-1938.

Brecknockshire	12,334		Denbighshire	7,166
Carmarthenshire	18,562		Flintshire	9,875 gain
Glamorganshire	262,060		Merionethshire	1,661
Monmouthshire	116,444		Montgomeryshire	8,470
Anglesey	5,050		Pembrokeshire	12,922
Caernarvonshire	834 gain		Radnorshire	3,268
Cardiganshire	2,433			

---

1 a) Explain the difference between immigration and emigration.
b) Why had Wales changed from a country attracting immigrants to a country exporting emigrants?
c) What effect did emigration have on Welsh society?

2 Study the statistics in source C.

a) Convert the figures into a bar graph. Indicate gains above the line and losses below the line.
b) In which two counties did the greatest losses occur?
c) Which two counties recorded population gains? In each case suggest possible reasons why this occurred.

LIFE IN THE DEPRESSION

Sport and Popular Entertainment

Despite the depression and unemployment, the years between the wars were full of opportunities for people to enjoy themselves. For the thousands with time on their hands, affordable leisure became an important feature of everyday life. They might go to the races to bet on the dogs or horses, to a football or rugby match, to clubs or to the free libraries to read books and newspapers. On the other hand, they might take advantage of modern technology to be entertained by the radio or gramophone or by a visit to the local cinema.

Radio

The first radios, popularly known as 'wireless' sets, appeared in Britain in 1922. At first they were expensive to buy, but within a few years mass production brought the price down to a level most people could afford. In 1926 the British Broadcasting Corporation (BBC) was set up to run the new national radio service.

Its task was to inform and entertain the listening public. This it did with a combination of live theatre, classical music and news programmes. Soon

SOURCE A

A front cover from the BBC's weekly *Radio Times* magazine.

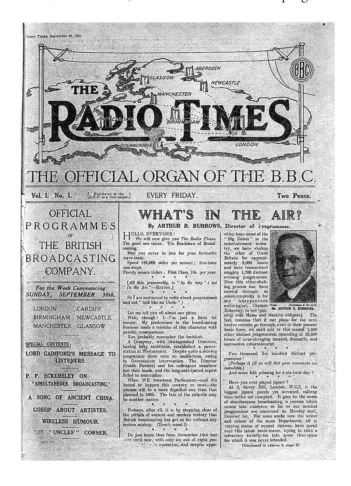

the BBC was broadcasting schools programmes, plays, popular music and comedy. Listeners were supposed to buy a license from the Post Office to pay for the service, at an average cost of 15s. (75p). Between 1929 and 1933 the sale of radio licenses doubled.

In 1937, after many years of asking, the BBC was persuaded to set up a Welsh service based in Cardiff to cater for the needs of Wales and its people. By 1939 nearly 75 per cent of British families owned a wireless set.

SOURCE B

Adapted from Professor Hughes's article, 'Wales and the BBC' in *Welsh Outlook*, a monthly magazine (1929).

In the autumn of 1928 I was making a brief [visit to] a Welsh village in Pembrokeshire. As a programme which I particularly desired to hear was due to be broadcast ... during my stay, I sought to ... listen in. The [hotel] ... and the homes of two or three of my acquaintances in the village [had] wireless sets, but in all cases they were out of [order] and had been in that state for varying periods. The explanation given was [that] they could not 'get' Cardiff and Swansea, while the London programmes ... contained too little that interested them to [be worth] the trouble and expense of keeping the sets going ... What Wales should demand is no more than the BBC ... has already granted to Scotland and Northern Ireland.

The Rise of Cinema

For the price of a 6d. (approximately 2p) ticket the cinema offered an escape from the harsh realities of life. Most of the films shown in British cinemas were American, made in Hollywood. Films stars like Clark Gable, Greta Garbo and Errol Flynn became famous across the world. It was the dream of every cinema-goer to meet their screen heroes or to become film stars themselves. During the 1930s one Welshman's dream became a reality. Raymond Truscott-Jones from Cadoxton in Neath left Wales to become famous as the Hollywood actor Ray Milland. As the popularity of the cinema soared so did the level of investment in films and buildings. By 1939 there were 4,776 cinemas in Britain, which sold on average nearly 23 million tickets per week.

SOURCE C

The famous novelist George Orwell commented on the powerful influence of cinema in his book, *Road to Wigan Pier* (1937).

In a decade of depression the ... two things that have probably made the greatest difference of all are the movies and the mass production of cheap smart clothes.
A youth of 20 for £2 10s. [£2.50] on h.p. [hire-purchase] can buy himself a suit ... the girl can look like a fashion plate [picture of a model] at even lower prices. You may have three half pence [less than 1p] in your pocket and not a prospect in the world, and only a corner of a leaky bedroom at home ... but in your new clothes you can stand on a street corner ... in a private day-dream of yourself as Clark Gable or Greta Garbo which compensates you [makes up for] a great deal.

SOURCE D

An advertising poster for the Palladium cinema in Pwllheli, North Wales (c. 1936).

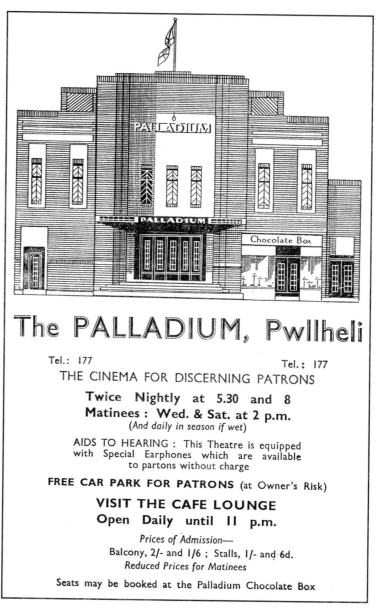

The PALLADIUM, Pwllheli

Tel.: 177   Tel.: 177

THE CINEMA FOR DISCERNING PATRONS

Twice Nightly at 5.30 and 8
Matinees : Wed. & Sat. at 2 p.m.
(And daily in season if wet)

AIDS TO HEARING : This Theatre is equipped with Special Earphones which are available to partons without charge

FREE CAR PARK FOR PATRONS (at Owner's Risk)

VISIT THE CAFE LOUNGE
Open Daily until 11 p.m.

Prices of Admission—
Balcony, 2/- and 1/6 ; Stalls, 1/- and 6d.
Reduced Prices for Matinees

Seats may be booked at the Palladium Chocolate Box

The BBC feared that cinema would replace radio as the most popular form of entertainment. In 1936 the BBC began live television broadcasts but this new form of entertainment 'cinema in the home' was far too expensive for most people. By 1939 there were only 50,000 viewers.

Sport

The three most popular sports in Wales were rugby, football and boxing. Boxing was the sport of the working classes and during the depression of the 1930s it became very popular. For many boxing provided the means to escape their poverty and unemployment. Local clubs arranged bouts for which the boxers were paid. The aim was to become a champion boxer but very few made it. Tommy Farr, an unemployed fairground fighter from Tonypandy, was perhaps the most successful Welsh boxer. He was remembered as 'the man who nearly beat Joe Louis', the world champion from America.

The late 1920s was the golden age of Welsh soccer. In 1927 Cardiff City won the FA cup followed in 1928 by Wales winning the Home

International Championship. The championship was clinched when the Reverend Hywel Davies, Vicar of Denbigh, scored the winning goal against the Irish! As a result of these victories people flocked to the grounds. However, when the Great Depression hit Wales, Welsh soccer suffered. In 1927 a broke Aberdare was forced to leave the Football League, while in 1931 Cardiff finished bottom of the Second Division. In 1935 Swansea Town was forced to launch a 'Save our Club' appeal and, in the same year, another Welsh club, Merthyr Tydfil, left the Football League. Yet, despite its lack of success, football continued to provide a release from the real world.

Welsh sports fans found little to cheer on the rugby field. Although club rugby was still strong the international team enjoyed only limited success. There were no Grand Slams and no Triple Crowns. As the depression deepened the number of talented rugby union players went north to play Rugby League. The two bright spots during the depression were the first victories over England at Twickenham and another win over the touring All Blacks in 1935. Wales beat New Zealand 13 – 12.

When they finished bottom of the Third Division in 1930, Merthyr [worked] hard for re-election but from nearly every English club whose vote could have saved them the answer was the same: 'Sorry, but we can't afford to keep you in.' Often, visiting clubs would leave Penydarren Park with less than £1 as their share of the 'gate' so when the vote was taken ... Thames United were elected instead.

SOURCE E

Peter Corrigan, 100 years of Welsh Soccer (1976).

STORY OF "MYSTERY" GOAL TOLD IN PHOTOGRAPHS.

SOURCE F

The winning goal for Cardiff in the FA Cup final. The headline in the *Western Mail* read 'When the Boys Come Marching Home' (25 April 1927).

---

1 Suggest reasons why the cinema was fast becoming the most popular form of entertainment during the 1930s?

2 a) What were the three most popular sports in Wales between the wars?
b) What effect did the depression have on these sports?

3 Why do you think that entertainments such as the cinema and radio were important during times of depression?

UNIT 1

Wales in Books; Wales on Film

Going to the cinema was by far the most popular form of mass entertainment in Wales in the 1930s. In 1934 it was calculated that in South Wales there was one cinema seat for every ten people and one for every 13 in North Wales. However, Welsh audiences were often fed a diet of American films made in Hollywood or British films made in London about England or the Empire. Few film studios were willing to produce films on Welsh subjects because they would struggle to be commercially successful. In any case the British government had the power to censor films that showed poverty and unemployment.

The few films that were made about Wales tended to ignore the country's social and economic problems. In the Hollywood film of *How Green Was My Valley* (1941), Richard Llewelyn's powerful novel of the harsh realities of life in a Welsh mining village was turned into a sentimental film of cosy lives and Welsh choral singing. There is little evidence of general suffering, ill-health or unemployment. The film was made in California where a Welsh village was built on a large Hollywood set. Almost without exception the star actors were Irish, Scottish or American. The only Welsh people in the film were the extras who formed the choirs.

However, there were some exceptional films. *The Citadel* explored the link between mining, poverty and ill-health. *The Proud Valley* is a film about a black American seeking work in a Welsh mine who eventually helps the locals save the mine from closure.

Writers and poets had more freedom to express themselves than film makers. The novels and poetry of the period well illustrate the problems that faced ordinary people in their everyday lives.

SOURCE A

Jack Jones, author and former miner from Merthyr, refers to the making of the film *The Proud Valley* by the Ealing Studios in London. *Western Mail* (1939).

> If it had been a film on any other subject I would not have come – not if you [Mr Balcon the producer] were to pay me thousands for it. But because you've got the courage to make a film about a piece of the country that's neglected and forgotten until another explosion or disaster awakens public interest for a day or two then I'll stay and work with you ... As a child I've covered dead men's faces down the mines. I've been sent to tell the women about the death of their men in the pit. I've been storing all these experiences up.

SOURCE B

A review of the film *The Stars Look Down* in *Liberty Magazine* (1941).

> This smashing film of Cronin's five-year-old novel of the Welsh coalfield could never have happened in Hollywood. It is grim, ruthless, full of the dark stenches of slimy mines ... It takes a savage crack at selfish capitalists ... MGM [an American film studio] acquired it, then hesitated to release it. Here it is two years later. It will never be box-office, but it is an outstanding achievement.

SOURCE C

(left) A scene from the film *How Green Was My Valley* (1941).

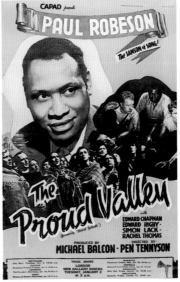

What will you do with your shovel, Dai,
And your pick and your sledge and your spike,
And what will you do with your leisure, man,
Now that you're out on strike?

What will you do for your butter, Dai,
And your bread and your cheese and your fags,
And how will you pay for a dress for the wife,
And shall your children go in rags?

You have been in your time a hero, Dai,
And they wrote of your pluck [courage] in the press,
And now you have fallen on evil days,
And who will be there to bless?

And how will you stand with your honesty, Dai,
When the land is full of lies,
And how will you curb your anger, man,
When your natural patience dies?

SOURCE D

(above) A poster advertising the film *The Proud Valley* (1939).

SOURCE E

(left) An extract from the poem 'The Angry Summer' by Idris Davies (1943).

OVERVIEW

Consider the following key question. In what ways and to what extent did changes in the economic fortunes of Wales and England affect people's lives in the 1930s?

1 a) **Explain what Jack Jones (source A) meant when he said that it took 'courage' to make a film of life in a Welsh mining community during the 1930s?**
b) **What did the reporter in source B mean when he said that the film *The Stars Look Down* 'will never be box-office'?**
c) **What do you learn from the text and from sources A and B about the** attitude of film-makers and film-making in general in the 1930s?

2 **What should historians be aware of if they use films such as *How Green Was My Valley* to investigate life in Wales in the 1930s?**

3 **How effective is Idris Davies' poem in representing the life of the average 'valleys Welshman'?**

UNIT 2

BRITAIN AND THE THREAT OF GERMANY

Democracy or Dictatorship?
The Changing Face of Europe

> **KEY ISSUE:**
> *Why did Britain go to war with Germany in 1939?*

In 1918 the British public greeted the news that the war had ended with almost uncontrollable joy; the years of fighting, killing and dying were over. People hoped and expected that the world would be a better and safer place. The post-war treaties – Versailles with Germany, St Germain with Austria, Neuilly with Bulgaria, Sevres with Turkey and Trianon with Hungary – were intended to secure a great peace. They were supposed to ensure that the defeated nations would never again be in a position to threaten anyone. A League of Nations was set up to support the idea of **collective security**, which meant that if one member nation was attacked the others would go to its aid. The victorious Allies – Britain, France and the USA – were confident that the idea of democracy would spread across Europe. They hoped it would establish itself in the new countries created by the treaties and in the defeated nations like Germany.

The Rise of Nationalism

At first all went well. There was a post-war economic boom. Germany, Austria, Poland and Czechoslovakia became free democracies and the Germans were allowed to join the League in 1926. The period 1924–9 is seen by some as a 'golden age' in European relations. Unfortunately, this did not last. The post-war treaties were unpopular and resented by the defeated nations which led them to seek revenge. This led to a growth in nationalism which in turn led some countries to adopt aggressive foreign policies. From 1933 one of the aims of German foreign policy under Hitler and the Nazis was to secure the return of all those territories taken away by the treaty of Versailles.

The League of Nations, led by Britain and France, was weak and indecisive. It failed to keep the peace. Powerful nations like the USA retreated into isolation and refused to join, while the Communist USSR was not trusted and became a member far too late to be of any use to the organisation. Soon even former allies like Italy were beginning to turn against the League and ignore its rules. In 1935 Italy invaded the African state of Abyssinia (modern Ethiopia) and, despite stern warnings from Britain, France and the League, the Italians conquered the country.

THE AWFUL WARNING.

FRANCE AND ENGLAND
(together ?).

"WE DON'T WANT YOU TO FIGHT,
BUT, BY JINGO, IF YOU DO,
WE SHALL PROBABLY ISSUE A JOINT MEMORANDUM
SUGGESTING A MILD DISAPPROVAL OF YOU."

SOURCE A

A cartoon from *Punch* (1935), showing Britain and France (as the League) warning Italy.

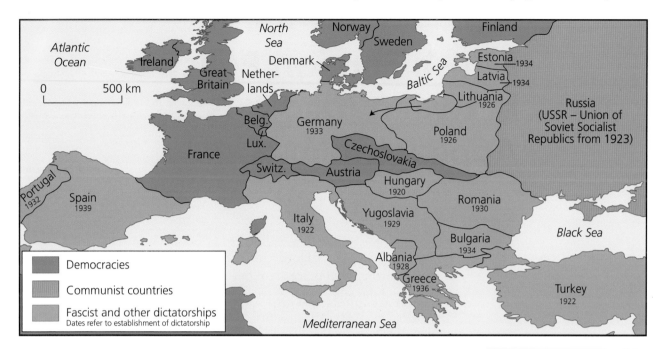

The democratic, fascist and communist countries of Europe by 1939.

From Prosperity to Slump

The economic boom after the First World War did not last. By 1923 most European countries, including Britain, were suffering. Weak and frequent changes of governments in the 1920s and 30s failed to cope with high inflation and rising unemployment. As a result, many people turned against the idea of democracy. This was particularly true of countries like Poland, Romania and Germany which had never experienced democracy before. To many Germans the pre-war **dictatorship** of **Kaiser** Wilhelm appeared strong and proud, while post-war democracy seemed to equal weakness, defeat and humiliation. As the economic situation got worse people became desperate. They turned to men like Hitler in Germany, Mussolini in Italy or Admiral Horthy in Hungary because they offered strong rule and promises to cure unemployment. Fascist and communist dictatorships like those in Italy and Russia began to spread throughout Europe.

1 What do the following terms mean:
   (i) democracy and (ii) dictatorship?

2 The following list contains features of democratic and fascist forms of government. Rearrange the statements under the headings 'democratic government' and 'fascist government':
   ● many political parties
   ● no secret police
   ● tolerates all political parties
   ● freedom of speech and of the media
   ● believes in discussion with other countries to solve problems
   ● pro-nationalist
   ● no freedom of speech and state control of the media
   ● secret police
   ● one-party state
   ● anti-communist

3 Study source B.
   a) List the countries that were:
   (i) democratic (ii) fascist and
   (iii) communist by 1939.
   b) Would you describe Europe in 1939 as: (i) mainly democratic or (ii) mainly dictatorships? Give a reason for your answer.

British Foreign Policy between the Wars: Appeasement

1919–29

From 1919 the aim of Lloyd George and his Coalition government was the maintenance of peace according to the terms of the Treaty of Versailles and the other post-war treaties. Although he knew that the treaties were far from perfect, Lloyd George was also aware that there was nothing to replace them.

The leader of the Labour government of 1924, Ramsay MacDonald, shared Lloyd George's desire to maintain peace but he was less certain about keeping to the terms of the post-war treaties. He believed that Germany had been harshly treated so he was in favour of a policy of **appeasement**. This aimed to avoid war by seeking conciliation rather than confrontation. MacDonald believed that the best way to keep the peace was not for Britain or France to act alone, but to work with their European partners in the League of Nations. He even restored diplomatic relations with the new Communist government of the USSR, an act for which he was criticised. Although only in power for a short period – January to October 1924 – there is no doubt that MacDonald, a strong believer in pacifism, played an important role in easing the tension that was building up in Europe.

In November 1924 the Conservative government of Stanley Baldwin cut Britain's diplomatic links with the USSR but continued MacDonald's policy of trying to replace the unfair terms of the post-war treaties with something better. The government was so confident that there would be no major European war for at least 10 or 15 years, if at all, that they cut expenditure on arms, reducing the size of the army and air force.

1929–35

By 1929 Britain, Germany, Italy and France were on very good terms. All were members of the League of Nations and all were convinced that diplomacy and friendly foreign relations were the keys to peace. During this period British public opinion had turned to support MacDonald's efforts to arrange a World Disarmament Conference. The Conference began in February 1932 and continued until April 1934, but it ended in complete failure. MacDonald had pinned his hopes on the success of the Conference, but he was let down by the French and Germans who failed to agree on almost every point. The new leader of Germany, Adolf Hitler (elected in 1933) used the failure of the Conference as an excuse to withdraw his country from the League of Nations.

Between 1930 and 1934 the international situation got worse. Mussolini promised the Italians an empire stretching across the Mediterranean into North Africa. Hitler promised the Germans peace, prosperity and pride and a German empire in the east. Most importantly, he promised to destroy the Treaty of Versailles by uniting all the Germans living in territories taken away by the treaty. These were as follows.

THE SAARLAND. This was a rich coal mining area which had been taken from Germany in 1919. At the beginning of 1935 the people of the Saar were given the freedom to vote on their future: unite with France, return to Germany or remain under League of Nations control. Over 90 per cent voted to return to Germany. This was a massive propaganda victory for Hitler.

THE RHINELAND. This large slice of Germany west of the Rhine had been de-militarised by the Treaty of Versailles.

AUSTRIA. Hitler was keen to unite the German-speaking peoples of Germany and Austria. Such a union was referred to as the *Anschluss*.

THE SUDETENLAND. The Sudeten area of Czechoslovakia was home to some 3 million Germans. Hitler claimed that they wished to become a part of Germany.

DANZIG. This important Baltic port had been taken away from Germany and made a free state under League of Nations and Polish control. Hitler claimed that the people of Danzig were being maltreated by the Poles and that they wished to become a part of Germany again.

THE POLISH CORRIDOR. Hitler claimed this area of Poland because it would give him access to Danzig and East Prussia.

"S-S-SHOULDN'T WE **DO** SOMETHING?"
"T-TOO RISKY! L-LET'S STAY HERE AND DEPLORE."

SOURCE A

'Mass murder in China'. A cartoon from the *Evening Standard* in 1937, showing Britain and the USA hiding while Japan attacks China.

A number of British politicians trusted Hitler and welcomed his rise to power. They thought he could be used to stop the spread of **communism.** Others saw him as a threat to world peace. One Conservative politician, Winston Churchill, attacked Hitler and called on the government to end the policy of appeasement. But he was ignored.

During this period MacDonald's military advisers urged him to abandon talks on disarmament and to rearm Britain in the face of Hitler's election as Chancellor of Germany in 1933. MacDonald refused. He claimed that the people of Britain remembered only too well the horrors of the last war and that they wanted to avoid fighting at all costs.

By 1935 even MacDonald was forced to agree that the League's idea of collective security had failed. He published 'A Statement Relating to Defence' which called for an increase in the size of the Royal Navy and the RAF. Hitler continued to ignore the Versailles treaty by introducing conscription, thus massively increasing the size of the German army. At the Stresa Conference in April 1935 MacDonald persuaded France and Italy to criticise Hitler for ignoring the terms of the Versailles treaty. With this success MacDonald hoped to isolate Germany but some of his ministers and senior advisers thought this policy was bound to lead to war. Instead the Anglo-German Naval Agreement was drawn up by which Britain agreed to allow Germany to increase the size of its navy, as long as it was limited to 35 per cent of that of Britain. This agreement went against traditional British foreign policy. Britain did not consult France and Italy, who felt betrayed. They would be less likely to trust the British in future.

SOURCE B

David Hill, *British History Study Guide*, 1914–51 (1993).

The mood of the country was ... pacific [for peace]. Dick Sheppard's Peace Pledge Union had 80,000 members soon after its founding in October 1934. The League of Nations Union Peace Ballot, in June 1935, showed the popular dislike of armaments. The East Fulham By-Election of October 1933, when a National Government candidate [calling for] more armaments was defeated by a Labour candidate opposed to it, was often [used] as evidence of the mood of the electorate [voters].

1935–7

One of the first problems the new Prime Minister, Stanley Baldwin, had to face was the Italian invasion of Abyssinia in north-east Africa in October. According to the rules of the League of Nations, countries like Britain and France could either attack Italy or impose economic **sanctions** if the Italians refused to withdraw. However, Britain and France were reluctant to punish Italy because they feared that Mussolini would join his one-time enemy Hitler. They tried to compromise with Mussolini but he ignored them. The limited sanctions that were applied against Italy were ineffective and they were withdrawn by the British in 1936.

By 1936 Hitler was convinced that the time was right to march into the Rhineland, a part of Germany which had been demilitarised by the Treaty of Versailles. He gambled and won, for no attempt was made to oppose the German army from occupying the area. At the same time Mussolini began to negotiate closer ties with Hitler. This new alliance was put to the test during the Spanish Civil War (1936–9). Although both Hitler and Mussolini had promised to keep out of the war, they did all they could, short of declaring war, to help the fascists win. After three years of bitter civil war, General Franco won and Spain became yet another fascist state.

By 1937 Baldwin was considering whether to begin to rearm Britain. Baldwin knew that although the British people were slowly beginning to change their views, pacifism was still popular while rearmament was not. Faced with such a decision, Baldwin resigned. He was succeeded as Prime Minister by Neville Chamberlain, who believed that he could maintain peace.

SOURCE C

A cartoon from the *Evening Standard* in 1935, showing Mussolini criticising the League of Nations.

TIMELINE OF KEY EVENTS LEADING TO THE OUTBREAK OF WAR

1931 – The League of Nations fails to prevent the Japanese invasion of Manchuria in China.

1933 – Hitler and the Nazis come to power in Germany.

1934 – The World Disarmament Conference ends in failure.
Germany withdraws from the League of Nations.
Hitler begins the rearmament of Germany.

1935 – Mussolini, dictator of Italy, orders the invasion of Abyssynia (Ethiopia).
The League of Nations fails to persuade the Italians to withdraw.

1936 – Hitler orders German troops to re-occupy the Rhineland.
Spanish Civil War breaks out. Hitler and Mussolini aid General Franco's fascist rebels.
Hitler and Mussolini become allies by signing the Rome-Berlin Axis.

1937 – Italy, Germany and Japan become allies by signing an anti-communist pact called the Rome-Berlin-Tokyo Axis.

1938 – Hitler orders German troops to invade Austria. Austria is united with Germany.
Britain and France agree to surrender the Sudeten area of Czechoslovakia to Hitler.

1939 – Hitler orders German troops to occupy the rest of Czechoslovakia.
Germany invades Poland.

1 a) What is meant by: (i) appeasement and (ii) collective security?
b) How did the failure of collective security contribute to the policy of appeasement?

2 Why were: (i) MacDonald and (ii) Baldwin reluctant to stand up to Germany and Italy?

BRITAIN AND THE THREAT OF GERMANY

Neville Chamberlain, Munich and the Drift to War

Historians in the past have blamed Chamberlain for the policy of appeasement that eventually failed and which led to world war. Today, however, many historians tend to sympathise with Chamberlain for the failure of a policy which he did not invent but inherited from prime ministers before him. They say it was not his fault that by 1938 the policy of appeasement was no longer working.

Chamberlain's Foreign Policy 1937–8

Having regained the Saar in 1935 and the Rhineland in 1936, Chamberlain hoped that Hitler would behave reasonably, abide by agreements and settle future disputes around the conference table. He was convinced that neither Hitler nor Mussolini wanted war and that they were as eager as him to keep the peace.

SUPPORT FOR APPEASEMENT

Chamberlain's policy had a great deal of support from the British public with its strong pacifist sympathies. In Parliament he was supported by the Labour Party. A number of politicians even admired Hitler for his work in curing unemployment and for having overcome the economic depression in Germany. In 1936 Lloyd George went so far as to meet Hitler in Germany, after which he publicly stated that the Chancellor was a man to be trusted. Chamberlain agreed and pointed out that since collective security under the League of Nations had failed there was no alternative to his policy. Some of his Conservative supporters still thought that the dictators could be used as a defence against the spread of communism from the USSR. There was still some sympathy for the view that the Germans had been badly treated at Versailles and that they had the right to be united under one flag. Another important consideration is the fact that Britain was simply not ready for war. It had only begun to rearm and was unable to defend itself from a determined attack. Indeed, the economic depression had *cut* the amount of money Britain was able to spend on arms and the army.

DOUBTS EMERGE

On the other hand, there was a growing concern in the country that Britain should have little to do with Hitler and Mussolini. They were fascist dictators who held power through fear and repression rather than by democratic means. Chamberlain's own cabinet was split; Lord Halifax supported Chamberlain's search for peace and the policy of appeasement but the Foreign Secretary, Sir Anthony Eden, believed that a firmer stand should be taken against Hitler and Mussolini. The most outspoken critic of appeasement was Winston Churchill who at this time was a **back-bench** Conservative MP. Few in government listened to him, but he was gaining support in the country for his view that war was inevitable unless Hitler was stopped.

AUSTRIA. In spite of Chamberlain's best efforts Hitler continued to press ahead with his aggressive foreign policy. In 1938 German troops forced their way into Austria. Hitler claimed that his German-speaking fellow countrymen wished to unite with Germany. Chamberlain protested but took no action.

CZECHOSLOVAKIA. This encouraged Hitler to go further and he began to demand self-determination for Germans living in the Sudeten area of Czechoslovakia. Hitler ordered Heinlein, leader of the Czech Germans, to mount marches and demonstrations demanding union with Germany. The Czech Prime Minister, Benes, was determined to resist Hitler and he asked the west to support him. Hitler threatened war.

A worried Chamberlain flew three times to Germany to meet Hitler. On 15 September he flew to Hitler's holiday home at Berchtesgaden in Bavaria for a general discussion over Hitler's demands. The result was British and French recognition of the Sudeten Germans' claim to self-determination. On 22 September, Chamberlain flew to Godesberg on the Rhine to discuss how best to settle the issue peacefully and without confronting the Czechs. Hitler, however, now demanded that the whole of Czechoslovakia be given to him. The meeting ended in deadlock. Chamberlain met the French leader and promised to support his plan to aid the Czechs in the event of war. The British fleet was mobilised, trenches were dug, sandbags were issued and air-raid precautions taken. War seemed inevitable. Finally, on 29 September 1938, in a desperate bid to avoid war, Chamberlain flew to Munich.

THE MUNICH CONFERENCE 1938

Chamberlain tried one final tactic and appealed to Mussolini for help. He gambled that although the Italian dictator had signed a treaty of alliance with Hitler, Mussolini was not ready for war. Chamberlain was right. Mussolini persuaded Hitler to meet the British Prime Minister, and a four-power conference (Italy, Germany, France and Britain) was arranged at Munich. Chamberlain and the French Prime Minister, Daladier, managed to persuade Hitler to sign an agreement which said that he could only take

A press photographer captures Chamberlain's triumphant return from Munich.

the Sudetenland. The four powers agreed to guarantee the independence of the rest of Czechoslovakia. Hitler and Chamberlain also signed a declaration which stated that they did not intend to go to war with one another. Chamberlain returned to Britain victorious and declared 'Peace in our time.' There was a general feeling of relief throughout Britain and Chamberlain was regarded as a national hero. But the Czech people felt betrayed.

The Drift to War: Czechoslovakia and Poland

In March 1939 German troops invaded and occupied the rest of Czechoslovakia. The Munich agreement had lasted barely six months before it collapsed. Chamberlain was genuinely shocked and he needed little persuasion to finally adopt a more militaristic policy; like MacDonald and Baldwin before him he was faced with a choice: appeasement or rearmament. Chamberlain pressed ahead with rearmament and by 1939 nearly 20 per cent of government expenditure went on arms and the armed forces. Some of Chamberlain's cabinet colleagues still firmly believed that Hitler could be reasoned with and that war could be avoided; Chamberlain grudgingly disagreed.

The British and French assured Poland of their full support should Hitler demand the return of the Polish corridor. They promised to declare war if German troops invaded. Lloyd George, Churchill and the Labour Party pressed the government for an alliance with the USSR. However, the Conservatives distrusted communism and although negotiations were opened with Stalin they never really had much chance of success. Stalin feared a German attack, but he also realised that the British and French could not be trusted, so in August Stalin and Hitler reached an agreement. The Nazi-Soviet Non-Aggression Pact shocked the world. Few could believe that these two bitter enemies were now friends. An invasion of Poland had become inevitable since Hitler was now certain that the USSR would not come to its aid. To the last Hitler gambled that Chamberlain and the French government would rather talk than fight and that if he invaded Poland they would not declare war. Hitler had been right so many times before but this time he was wrong.

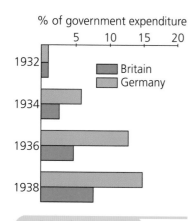

% of government expenditure

SOURCE A

Military spending 1932–8 (as a percentage of government expenditure).

SOURCE B

Adapted from A.J.P. Taylor's *English History 1914–1945* (1965).

Hitler's decision for war. It is not clear why Hitler made this decision. Of course there is no problem for those who regard Hitler as either a madman or as set on a world war all along. But these views do not take account of his previous behaviour. Hitler had been a skillful, though [untrustworthy], negotiator and had carried Germany nearer to domination of Europe by threats and bluff. His military preparations also seem to suggest that he intended further bluffs, or, at worst, brief wars against minor opponents. It is hard to believe that he wanted a full-scale war against Great Britain and France. [I am inclined to think] he misjudged the situation.

SOURCE C

Hitler's territorial demands and gains, 1936–9.

He [Hitler] gave his word that he would respect the Locarno Treaty; he broke it. He gave his word that he neither wished nor intended to annex [take over] Austria; he broke it. He declared that he would not incorporate [take over] the Czechs into the Reich [Empire]; he did so. He gave his word after Munich that he had no further territorial demands in Europe; he broke it. He gave his word that he wanted no Polish provinces; he broke it. He has sworn to you for years that he was the mortal enemy of Bolshevism [Communist Russia]; now he is its ally.

SOURCE D

Prime Minister Chamberlain explains in a radio broadcast to the German people why he has declared war, 4 September 1939.

?

1 a) List what you think were the five most important reasons for appeasing Hitler.
   b) On returning from Munich Chamberlain declared 'In war there are no winners, but all are losers.' What might Hitler have thought about Chamberlain's foreign policy as a result?

2 Study the text and sources A, B, C and D. Do you think Hitler intended to go to war with Britain and France?

3 Why was Chamberlain regarded as:
   (i) a national hero in September 1938?
   (ii) a failure in September 1939?
   Explain your answers.

4 Do you think Chamberlain should be partly blamed for the outbreak of the Second World War? Give reasons for your answer.

The Reactions of the British Press to Hitler and Appeasement

SOURCE A

A cartoon from 1936.

THE GOOSE-STEP.

"GOOSEY GOOSEY GANDER,
WHITHER DOST THOU WANDER!"
"ONLY THROUGH THE RHINELAND—
PRAY EXCUSE MY BLUNDER!"

SOURCE B

'Increasing Pressure' – a cartoon by David Low,
18 February 1938.

SOURCE C

'Stepping Stones to Glory' – a cartoon by
David Low, 8 July 1936.

SOURCE D

'Nightmare Waiting List' – a cartoon by David Low, 9 September 1938.

SOURCE E

This cartoon from September 1938 shows Neville Chamberlain trying to steer the world towards peace.

SOURCE F

One view of the Munich Agreement. A cartoon from the *Daily Worker*, a communist newspaper, 1 October 1938.

1 **What are the strengths and weaknesses of cartoons as sources of historical information?**

2 **Why do you think these cartoons would have been popular with the British public?**

3 **Look at source A. What information does it contain to suggest that Hitler could not be trusted?**

4 **What was the cartoonist David Low predicting would happen in source C?**

5 **What events are referred to in the cartoons published in 1938?**

6 **Explain the reactions of the British press to Chamberlain's policy of appeasement.**

BRITAIN AND THE THREAT OF GERMANY

Fascism and the British People

During the 1920s most Britons cared little about events in Europe or the rest of the world. Few people took much notice of Mussolini's rise to power in Italy in 1922 – they were more concerned about the economic depression and rising unemployment at home. According to one contemporary commentator, Charles Masterman, 'England is not interested in anything at all ... It is like a sick man resting after a great outletting of blood. The nervous system is dead.' They did not want to get involved in another war but neither, it seems, did they care if the League of Nations succeeded or failed.

The mood of the people began to change by the beginning of the 1930s. The rise of Hitler in Germany frightened many people, and memories of the First World War when Germany had been the enemy, were still fresh. However, there were Britons who firmly believed that **fascism** or communism was not a threat.

Founded in 1930 by an ex-Labour MP Sir Oswald Mosley, the British Union of Fascists (BUF) modelled itself on Mussolini's Italian *Fascisti*. It took the BUF only 18 months to attract a membership of 20,000. By 1934 Mosley had turned to supporting Hitler and British fascists were soon adopting the Hitler salute, becoming anti-Jewish and wearing black uniforms. BUF branches were established across the country including four in Wales – at Cardiff, Swansea, Newport and Merthyr Tydfil. In June 1934 there was a clash between fascists and communists in London which led to

SOURCE A

Sir Oswald Mosley (middle of front row) inspects a British Union of Fascists (BUF) guard of honour at a rally in 1935.

serious rioting. There were riots in Ebbw Vale, Aberdare and Pontypridd but the most serious occurred at Tonypandy where 2,000 people demonstrated against a proposed BUF rally. Unemployment, economic depression, nationalism, racism, boredom and thuggishness and the attraction of brawling were responsible for attracting people to extreme views. In this atmosphere a number of people turned towards skilled and charismatic leaders like Mosley.

However, even at its height in 1937 the BUF was never very popular; it could only raise a membership figure of 30,000. The voters of Wales and Scotland mainly continued to support the Labour Party. During the 1930s it had little support in England where the Conservative Party and the National Government it dominated, enjoyed massive support. Voters tended to support the policy of appeasement – although this changed after 1938 when even the British public realised that only force could possibly stop Hitler. As war approached, membership of the BUF began to fall. When war was declared Mosley and the BUF leadership were arrested and membership of the BUF was declared illegal.

The Response of Welsh Nationalists

Although few Welshmen joined the British fascist movement there were some members of the Welsh Nationalist Party *(Plaid Cymru)* like Ambrose Bebb who were pro-Mussolini. Others were openly anti-English, but they all shared a belief in pacifism. According to Professor Kenneth Morgan 'There were Welshmen who accused *Plaid Cymru* of the same kind of racialism and ... nationalism associated with the Nazi and fascist parties of Germany or Italy.' In fact, during the war the German secret service considered contacting some members of *Plaid Cymru* in order to gain their support in the event of an invasion! The invasion never came and the loyalty of some of *Plaid Cymru's* members was never put to the test. By 1945 the party was firmly established and it came to play a more significant role in the political and cultural life of post-war Wales.

> ... [the war] is a clash of rival imperialisms from which Wales, like the other small nations of Europe, has nothing to gain but everything to lose ... It does not accept the popular English view that this is a crusade of light against darkness. It does not admit the right of England to conscript Welshmen into her army or regard it as the duty of Wales to help London beat Berlin.

SOURCE B

A British anti-fascist pamphlet, published in 1934.

SOURCE C

Professor J.E. Daniel, president of *Plaid Cymru*, quoted in the *Western Mail* in August 1940.

1 **Why might some people have considered Professor Daniel's article in the *Western Mail* (source C) to be: (i) courageous (ii) foolish?**

2 **Why did the membership of the BUF: (i) increase so rapidly during the early 1930s but (ii) decline so quickly after 1939?**

OVERVIEW

Consider the following key question. Why did Britain go to war with Germany in 1939?

Penyberth and Welsh Nationalism

The growth of nationalism that was so much a feature of the period between the wars was not confined to continental Europe; Wales too had its nationalists. Well known poets, writers, lecturers and teachers lent their support to both nationalist and cultural movements, beginning in 1922 with the founding of the *Urdd Gobaith Cymru*. This was a youth organisation aimed at saving the Welsh language and culture. The movement was a success, claiming some 5,000 members in 1927 rising to an estimated 50,000 by 1934.

Soon Welsh intellectuals like Saunders Lewis, W. Ambrose Bebb and J.E. Daniel came to the conclusion that the only way to save Welsh culture and the Welsh way of life was by gaining independence. They also realised that to achieve their aim they needed a political voice and political power. So at the Pwllheli *Eisteddfod* in 1925 they founded a political party, the Welsh Nationalist Party or *Plaid Cymru*. Support for the party grew very slowly; there were 500 members in 1930 rising to 2,000 by 1939.

The nationalists attacked men like Lloyd George and D.A. Thomas (see pages 40–41 and 66–69) whom they saw as traitors because they refused to support Welsh independence. These public attacks gained much needed publicity but in Saunders Lewis's view it was not enough. In 1936 he planned to strike a blow against the 'English' government that would send shock waves throughout Wales. Saunders Lewis, the Rev. Lewis Valentine and D. J. Williams burnt down part of the RAF training school at Penyberth near Pwllheli. The aim was to gain maximum publicity and public sympathy for the nationalist cause.

After the fire the three gave themselves up to the police. They were tried in Caernarfon but the jury could not agree on a verdict. They were then tried in London, found guilty of arson and jailed for a year.

SOURCE A

Saunders Lewis speaking in 1936.

My firm opinion is this – that it is necessary also to break every link with the Parliament in England. That is essential to the success of our objectives [aims]. The Nationalist Party must work in Wales through the local authorities, making Wales Welsh through them, and leaving the Parliament of England alone, boycotting [ignoring] Parliament, and thereby making a Welsh Wales a fact ... Nothing will ever come to Wales through the Parliament of England ... The Welsh language must be the only official language of Wales ... The Welsh Nation must gain its political freedom without resort to violence. And I submit to you that our action in burning the Penrhos Aerodrome proves the sincerity of this affirmation [declaration].

SOURCE B

The Rev. Lewis Valentine, Swansea University lecturer Saunders Lewis and school teacher D.J. Williams in 1936.

I no longer consider myself a member of *Plaid Cymru* ... I know of no-one who has done more for Wales than Mr D. Lloyd George. Indeed, the wide world would know nothing of Wales were it not for Mr Lloyd George. There is no more secure leader for Wales than Mr Lloyd George and great benefits have come to Wales through him. He has served his own nation by serving the world as every true patriot should. It is high time that we Welsh should be loyal to one another and to our best men instead of fighting amongst ourselves.

SOURCE C

An extract from a private letter (undated) from Mr J.R. Jones, a member of the party, to Mr H.R. Jones, a party official. J.R. Jones is complaining about the party's decision to contest its first election in Caernarvonshire, an area loyal to David Lloyd George.

The aim of *[Plaid Cymru]* was not originally to get self-government for Wales, [but] **dominion** status ... on the same footing as Canada or Australia. The immediate concern was to ensure the future of the Welsh language. *Plaid Cymru* did not have much impact immediately. Then in 1936 came an event which focused attention on the Party ... [Penyberth, but] there was no long term increase in membership of the Party ...

SOURCE D

Gareth E. Jones, *People, Protest and Politics: Case Studies in Twentieth-Century Wales* (1987).

SOURCE E

A map of Wales showing the results of the Welsh Nationalist Party parliamentary election campaigns, 1925–45. Also see source F on page 125.

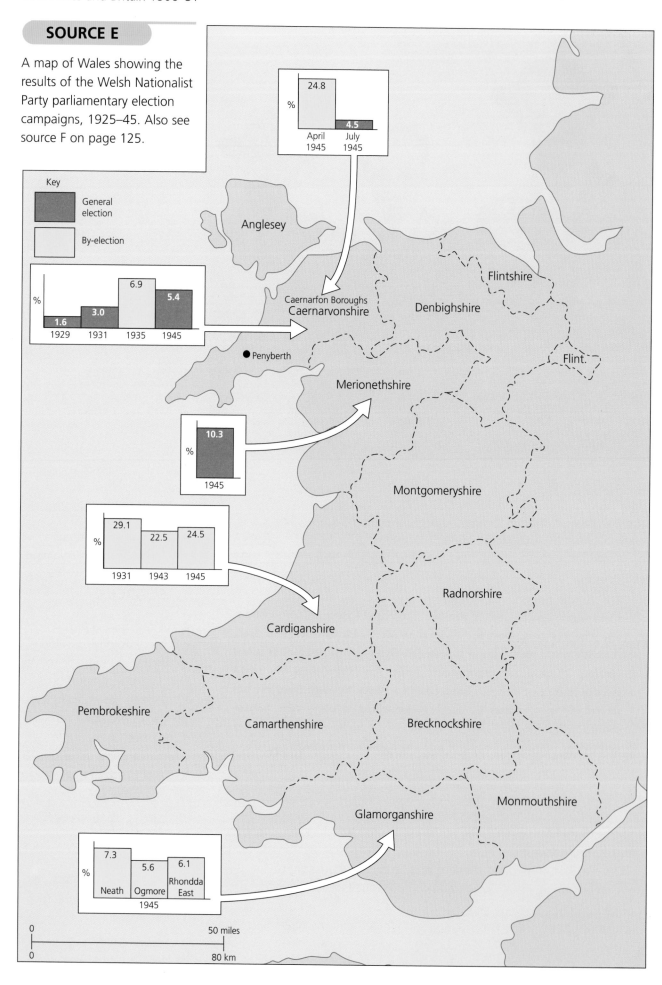

Key

■ General election

□ By-election

April 1945: 24.8% July 1945: 4.5%

1929: 1.6 1931: 3.0 1935: 6.9 1945: 5.4

Caernarfon Boroughs
Caernarvonshire

● Penyberth

Anglesey

Flintshire

Denbighshire

Flint.

Merionethshire

1945: 10.3%

Montgomeryshire

Radnorshire

1931: 29.1 1943: 22.5 1945: 24.5

Cardiganshire

Pembrokeshire

Camarthenshire

Brecknockshire

Monmouthshire

Glamorganshire

Neath: 7.3 Ogmore: 5.6 Rhondda East: 6.1
1945

0 — 50 miles

0 — 80 km

The results of the Welsh Nationalist Party parliamentary election campaigns, 1925–45. Adapted from D.H. Davies, The Welsh Nationalist Party, 1925–45 (1983).

Welsh Nationalist Party parliamentary election campaigns 1925–45				
Constituency	Date	Candidate	Vote	%
Caernarvonshire	May 1929	L. E. Valentine	609	1.6
Caernarvonshire University of Wales	Oct. 1931	J.E. Daniel Saunders Lewis	1,136 914	3.0 29.1
Caernarvonshire	Nov. 1935	J.E. Daniel	2,534	6.9
University of Wales	Jan. 1943	Saunders Lewis	1,330	22.5
Caernarfon Boroughs Neath	April 1945 May	J.E. Daniel Wynne Samuel	6,844 6,290	24.8 16.2
Caernarvonshire Caernarfon Boroughs Merionethshire Neath Ogmore Rhondda East University of Wales	July 1945	W. Ambrose Bebb J.E. Daniel Gwynfor Evans Wynne Samuel Trefor Morgan J. Kitchener Davies Dr Gwenan Jones	2,152 1,560 2,448 3,659 2,379 2,123 1,696	5.4 4.5 10.3 7.3 5.6 6.1 24.5

An extract from a letter from Lloyd George to his daughter Megan, December 1936.

Your ... telegram as to the action taken by the government in reference to the bombing school incident gave me a great shock. I think it is a piece of insolence, but very characteristic of the government. They crumple up when tackled by Mussolini and Hitler, but they take it out on the smallest country in the realm which they are misgoverning. It is the way cowards try to show that they are strong by bullying. They run away from anyone powerful enough to stand up to them and they take it out of the weak.

This is the first government that has tried Wales at the Old Bailey [London]. I wish I were there, and I certainly wish I were 40 years younger. I should be prepared to risk a protest which would be a defiance.

[It] is an outrage that makes my blood boil. It has nothing to do with my views as to the merits of the case. It will reinforce the pacifist movement in England.

1 a) What were the aims of the Welsh Nationalist Party?
b) Why did the party make personal attacks on the likes of such well-known Welshmen as Lloyd George, D.A. Thomas and Lord Rhondda?

2 Study sources C and F.
a) By using the information in source F suggest a date when Mr J.R. Jones's letter (source C) might have been written.
b) Why do you think *Plaid Cymru* concentrated their efforts to elect their first MP in the county of Caernarvonshire?

3 Read source G carefully.
a) What do you think Lloyd George meant when he said that Wales was being tried at the Old Bailey in London?
b) Why was Lloyd George so outraged by the court case involving Lewis, Valentine and Williams?
c) What does this extract tell us about Lloyd George and his 'Welshness'?

4 a) Explain the meaning of the word 'martyr'.
b) Do you believe Saunders Lewis, Lewis Valentine and D.J. Williams should be considered martyrs or criminals? Give reasons for your answer.

UNIT 3

Britain Goes to War, 1939

> **KEY ISSUE:**
> *How did people in Wales and England cope with the experiences of the Second World War?*

On 1 September 1939 Hitler invaded Poland. Two days later and for the second time in less than 30 years, Britain (along with France) declared war on Germany. Technology was to play a big role in the fighting. As the war continued, both sides built new and improved aeroplanes, both fighters and bombers, faster and deadlier tanks, bigger and better ships and submarines, missiles, rockets and jet aircraft. The USA and Britain designed and the USA developed the atomic bomb. The Second World War cost more lives than any other.

SOURCE A

The following people were interviewed on a television programme and asked to recall their memories. From *The Day War Broke Out* (1989).

(i) Mrs Buckland of London
They had said that war had been declared, and then the sirens [air raid warnings] went. We were petrified. Anyhow, some time afterwards, we were waiting for the guns to go, but we didn't hear anything, so that was the first day of the war. It was quite an exciting morning really, but it was sad to think that we were now at war.

(ii) Mr Barsley of Oxford
Well September 3 1939, I looked up my diaries that I was still a pacifist then, at the outbreak of war, and I noted that when I heard the tired voice of Chamberlain announcing that we were at war, I thought, this is it, this is the end of a long journey, which has taken the wrong turning, and I am dead against it.

(iii) Mrs Barnicott of Plymouth
We had planned a family party ... but of course it was cancelled ... my husband to be and my father spent the ... day digging a hole to put an Anderson [air raid] shelter in. My parents were more upset than we were, because they had come through the other war, so they knew more, they weren't so ignorant about it as we were.

(i) Mrs Reason of Cardiff
When the second world war started, the coalman said the valleys had come alive. The war meant jobs, everyone up there was jumping for joy because they'd get their money regularly.

(ii) Mr Jones of Ammanford
I remember that we all cheered. We were young lads, teenagers, it all seemed like a big adventure. We couldn't wait to join up. If only we'd known what lay ahead.

SOURCE B

An extract from *The Experiences of Wales in the Depression* (1986).

Another War to End all Wars?

Unlike the First World War, people knew that this war would probably not be over by Christmas. Large numbers of men and women 'joined up' but even more were conscripted either into the armed forces or into industry. However, this was a war in which civilians would be involved more closely than ever before, a fact that was brought home to them by the new air raid precautions and the plans for mass **evacuation** of the cities. Few people dared to hope that this would be a war to end all wars.

SOURCE C

The pacifists spread their message of peace.

SOURCE D

People march in protest.

1 Why were: (i) selling pacifist newspapers (source C) and (ii) protest marches (source D) made illegal within weeks of the war breaking out?

2 a) On hearing the news that war had been declared Mr Barsley said 'this is it, this is the end of a long journey, which has taken the wrong turning'. What do you think he meant by this? (Refer to the previous unit to help you.)
b) Why were Mrs Barnicott's parents more upset than she was at the news of war breaking out?

c) Why do you think the people of the Welsh valleys were either 'jumping for joy' or 'cheering' and wishing to 'join up to fight' when they heard that war had been declared?

3 a) What was the attitude of the people in this chapter to the news that war had broken out?
b) Do you believe that the opinions and attitudes expressed in these pages are representative of the attitudes of the British people across the country? Explain your answer.

The Second World War in Europe, 1939–45

On land the period from late September 1939 until April 1940 became known as the Phoney War because neither side felt confident enough to attack the other. Poland had surrendered after four weeks of fighting Germany alone. Britain's contribution to the Polish war effort had been to 'bomb' Germany with propaganda leaflets. But at sea the situation was quite different. British merchant ships were attacked by German submarines while the Royal Navy sank the German battleship *Graf Spee* in December 1939.

The Phoney War ended suddenly in April 1940 when Hitler invaded Denmark and Norway. British and French troops were sent to help the Norwegians but they were eventually defeated after nine weeks of fighting. In the meantime the Germans had launched a massive attack in the west against Holland, Belgium and France. The attack was carried out with large numbers of fast-moving tanks and planes. This **Blitzkrieg**, or 'lightning war' of the Germans proved decisive. The Dutch surrendered after four days, the Belgians lasted 18 days and the French asked for peace terms after six weeks. By 22 June 1940 it was all over. However, although the British and French armies had been smashed in the field they managed to escape capture. The so-called 'miracle' of Dunkirk was the rescue of around 338,000 Allied troops from the beaches of Normandy.

Britain Alone, 1940

SOURCE A

Hitler's main military successes, 1939–42.

Hitler planned to invade Britain but he needed control of the air in order to protect his troop ships as they crossed the English Channel. The Battle of Britain was an air war fought between July and October 1940 and it saw

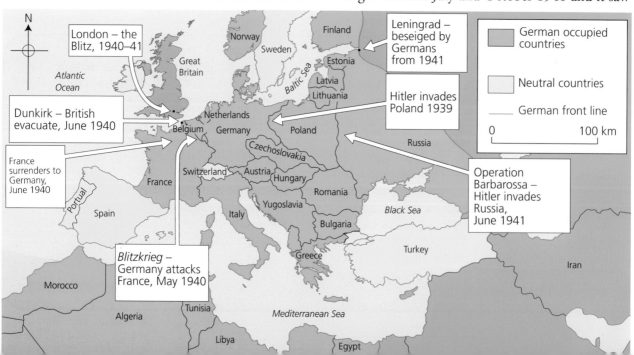

the first major British success of the war. Although heavily outnumbered the RAF managed to defeat the Luftwaffe and so prevent an invasion. However, it could not stop massive German bombing raids on a number of British cities – the **Blitz** – some of the worst hit being London, Coventry and Swansea (see pages 130–133).

Elsewhere, from 1939 until 1942 the German armies won one victory after the other. They seemed almost invincible. The British had easily defeated Mussolini's Italian armies in North Africa during 1940 but the desert war turned against them once German troops under General Rommel arrived to help their ally. In early 1941 Germany defeated Yugoslavia and Greece in a matter of weeks. Help from their British ally was too little too late.

The USSR Enters the War, 1941

The tide began to turn in Britain's favour from June 1941 when Hitler invaded the USSR. The British now had an ally against Germany. At first all went well for the Germans; their *Blitzkrieg* tactics seemed destined to succeed once again. Within six months of invasion they had defeated, killed or captured over 5 million Russians. They were besieging the country's second largest city, Leningrad, and they were only 19 miles from the capital Moscow. However, a combination of freezing winter weather, the huge size of the country and the grim determination of the Russian people to resist the invaders began to take its toll on the unprepared and outnumbered Germans.

The Grand Alliance, 1941–45

Germany's fate was sealed in December 1941 when the USA entered the war on the side of the Allies. The 'grand alliance' of Britain, the USA and USSR proved too powerful for Germany. Known as the 'arsenal of democracy', America had the wealth, manpower and industrial capacity to win the war. Soon US ships were supporting the Royal Navy in the Atlantic war which Britain had to win if it was to survive. German U-Boats had very nearly cut off Britain's supplies of food, oil and raw materials from the USA and the countries of the Empire.

By 1944 the Allies had won a number of decisive victories against the enemy. In October 1942 the British under General Montgomery defeated the Germans at El Alamein to begin to win the desert war in North Africa. The Russians crushed the German Sixth Army at Stalingrad in January 1943 and destroyed many of their tanks in the biggest tank battle in history at Kursk, in July 1943. Later that same month British and American forces invaded Italy, which led to the surrender of Germany's ally in September 1943. On D-Day, 6 June 1944, the Allies launched the biggest invasion in history when they landed at Normandy in France. The outnumbered German armies in France, Italy and Russia were in full retreat. By May 1945 Hitler was dead and the war in Europe was over.

El Alamein	Oct.	1942
Stalingrad	Jan.	1943
Surrender of North African Army	May	1943
Kursk	July	1943
Normandy	July–Aug.	1944
Battle of the Bulge	Jan.	1945
Battle of Berlin	April–May	1945

SOURCE B

A list of Hitler's military defeats, 1942–45.

? **1 What was the 'grand alliance'?**   **2 Why did Germany eventually lose the war?**

The Blitz

After the fall of France in June 1940 the British government warned its people to expect the worst: a massive bombing campaign against the ports and cities. They were wrong. Although Hitler gave the order for a concentrated air offensive against Britain on 31 July to be followed by an invasion in September, the Luftwaffe's main targets were the airfields of the RAF's fighter command and British shipping in the English Channel. Clearing the Channel of British warships followed by control of the air above it would enable the German invasion force to carry out its task. The Battle of Britain had begun.

The Battle of Britain

The Battle of Britain was fought high above the countryside of southern England, watched by local people. The RAF was heavily outnumbered, having a little over 1,200 fighter planes to combat 4,550 Luftwaffe aircraft. In the first five weeks of the battle the RAF lost nearly 20 per cent of its strength. In one week alone 185 Spitfires and Hurricanes had been destroyed. The German losses were just as heavy but they pressed ahead in the belief that the RAF could not hold out much longer. They were right – but the RAF was saved from total destruction when the Germans changed their tactics to bombing cities instead of airfields. On 7 September a furious Hitler ordered the Luftwaffe to bomb London in retaliation for the RAF bombing Berlin. The Blitz had begun.

The Targets of the Blitz

Hitler ordered his bombers to concentrate their efforts on destroying Britain's industry and its towns and cities of which London was the

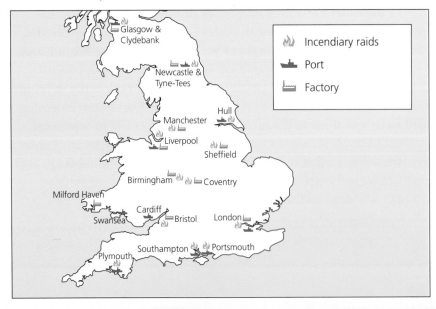

SOURCE A

The main urban and industrial targets of the Blitz.

main target. He hoped to force the British government to surrender by continuously bombing civilians and damaging their morale. London was bombed every night from 7 September to 2 November – about 13,561 tons of high-explosive bombs were dropped in 57 raids. Soon other cities were suffering mass bombing. On 14 November 1940 Coventry was raided for the first time. In that one night 554 people were killed, 50,000 houses and hundreds of shops were destroyed. Over the next two days German bombers returned to bomb what was left of the city.

In the face of growing losses of bomber planes the Germans switched to night bombing. With this came new incendiary bombs which caused massive fires. On one night alone – 29 December 1940 – fire bombs caused over 1,300 fires to break out in the centre of London. In 1941 the Germans began to range further afield, bombing Belfast, Glasgow, Swansea, Cardiff and Liverpool which was hit for eight nights in May causing the deaths of 2,000 civilians. On 31 May 1941 the Germans accidentally bombed Dublin, the capital of a neutral country.

The Blitz lasted from September 1940 until May 1941 during which 45,000 civilians were killed and 3.5 million houses were either damaged or destroyed. For every civilian killed, 35 were made homeless.

Coping with the Blitz

From the very first day of the war the government had planned for the expected mass bombing. It had set up civilian defence units like the Air Raid Precaution (ARP) wardens, the Auxiliary Fire Service, the First Aid posts and Ambulance Service. The civilian population had also been given instructions on how to protect themselves by using air raid shelters. The Anderson shelter consisted of sheets of metal set in earth and covered by soil while the Morriston shelter was a large steel box to be set up in the home, usually under the stairs. There were also communal shelters for large numbers of people. Londoners were fortunate enough to be able to use the underground.

At first the continuous night-time bombardment of Britain's cities and the heavy casualties it caused damaged morale. Churchill did what he could to raise people's spirits by his stirring and patriotic radio broadcasts and by touring the damaged areas. Government censorship meanwhile ensured that newspapers were not allowed to show pictures of dead bodies, and radio and cinema were told to concentrate on stories about the heroism of the rescue services. Fear, hate, destruction and government propaganda all contributed to an increased community spirit, a feeling of togetherness. The British people were determined to show Hitler that they could not be beaten and they tried to carry on with their daily lives as normally as possible.

SOURCE B

The *Daily Mail* reports on the bombing of a house in the outskirts of London.

SOURCE C

'After the raid – "Is it all right now, Henry?"
"Yes, not even scratched"'.
A cartoon from the *Daily Express* showing an Anderson shelter (1940).

1 a) **What were the aims of the German Blitz on Britain?**
b) **Did the Blitz succeed? Explain your answer.**

2 a) **What was the purpose of the report by the *Daily Mail* in source B?**
b) **What do you learn from the cartoon (source C) about the attitude of the British people to the Blitz?**

Swansea and the Three Nights' Blitz

For three nights, in February 1941, 250 German aircraft raided Swansea, dropping 1,320 high explosive bombs and around 56,000 incendiaries. The aim of the raid had been to destroy the town's docks and heavy industrial plants, but the Germans missed their targets and bombed the centre of Swansea instead. The incendiaries caused fires that could be seen as far away as Pembrokeshire and north Devon. Almost 400 people were killed, and many of the town's buildings were destroyed. Cardiff too had suffered and in one raid alone, on 2 January 1941, 151 men, 147 women and 47 children had been killed while some 600 houses had been destroyed. The war had come to Wales.

SOURCE A

The pilot's eye view from a German aircraft.

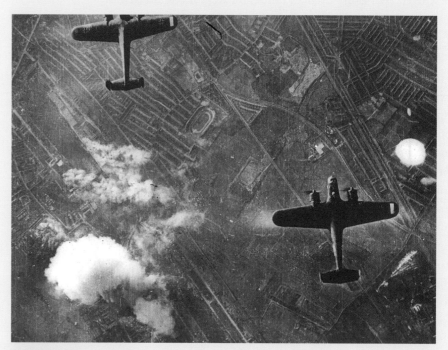

SOURCE B

A photograph taken by the *South Wales Evening Post* showing the bomb damage to the centre of Swansea in 1941.

(i) Mr Fifield
We lived in Greenfield Street throughout the war and we were right in the middle of it all. My family spent night after night in the concrete shelter opposite our house. I remember going up to St Mary's to try and get the candlesticks and other articles out of the church. We went through it all and never had a cracked window in the house. We also had laughter at different things that happened ... one night the warning went and the warden shouted 'Take cover'. One man dived under a van in Wassall Square. After it was all over, we saw the van on [the other side] of the Square and the man still on the road quite safe. I am now 80 years of age and I don't think that we will ever experience another time like that again. Not five minutes' walk from our house they flattened everything.

(ii) Mr Mansell
I was one of the first 20 ARP [Air Raid Precaution] wardens in Swansea. My ARP post was in Pottery Street that was bombed and then in Powell Street. One of the raids came when a messenger lad and I were on patrol, and bombs dropped ... hitting a house in Cwm Terrace and Philaparts Lodging House. I sent my messenger lad to the post and started to get some of the men out. My messenger came back and helped until the rescue team arrived. Out of the 48 we managed to get 42 out alive. The messenger lad, Jack Evans, was awarded the Boy Scout's highest award for bravery.

(iii) Mrs Jenkins
My brother's wife lost three members of her family by a direct hit on their shelter in Bryn-Syfi Terrace in the February Blitz. After the burial, we went to the cemetery to see the grave. I was amazed to see five or six open graves, and soldiers still digging other graves. On asking one of the soldiers who all the graves were for, he replied: 'They are ready for the next Blitz.'

(iv) Mr Pelzer
I was in the Home Guard and was detailed [ordered] to look after the Post Office in Llansamlet when the Blitz started. People were being brought in from the street to shelter from the shrapnel that was falling from the anti-aircraft guns. One such lady came into my care. I married her in 1945 after we both served in the forces ... and I've got to thank the Blitz for being blessed with three lovely daughters and six grandchildren. I've been blitzed for 42 years with happiness from them all.

SOURCE C

(left) These extracts from 'Memories of Swansea at war' were published by the *South Wales Evening Post* in 1988.

SOURCE D

(above) This photograph was taken the morning after a raid.

SOURCE E

(above) This photograph of St Mary's Church, Swansea was taken on 28 February 1941, a week after the end of the Blitz.

1 a) Why did the Germans bomb Swansea?
b) What effect did the bombing have on civilian life in the city?

2 Why did the government censor allow the photographs in sources D and E to be published but not the photograph in source B?

Life in Wartime Britain

In 1939 most Britons over the age of 35 remembered the previous war, so they had a fair idea of what to expect: shortages, censorship, rationing and sacrifice. However, although they were aware of the dangers of aerial bombing few were prepared for the Blitz which led to the destruction of towns, cities, factories and homes. Even fewer were prepared for the deaths of thousands of ordinary civilians – men, women and children regardless of age or class. The mass bombing of civilian targets was a terror largely unknown in the First World War and despite the use of anti-aircraft guns there was no real defence against it except for evacuation. Civilians of all ages quickly realised that this was a new kind of warfare where they were in danger of being killed.

Evacuation

SOURCE A

These posters were issued by the government in 1940.

SOURCE B

The *Daily Mail* report on the debate in Parliament about whether to make evacuation compulsory, June 1940.

When war was declared the government put its plan for evacuation into action. Evacuation was not compulsory because the government feared that people might protest at being forced to leave their homes or their children. Therefore, from the very beginning of the war evacuation was always voluntary but very much encouraged. The government wanted to avoid women and children being killed because this would affect morale. The plan was for all women and children to be evacuated from targets like London to safe areas such as Wales. Wales was thought to be safe because it was mainly rural and it had fewer military targets than England. Although most of the evacuees who came to Wales came from London and Birmingham, many Welsh women and children from Swansea and Cardiff were also evacuated to towns and villages in the country.

Some children were even sent abroad to Canada and the USA. In a number of cases only children were evacuated because their parents had important city jobs which were vital for the war effort. In other cases, those who refused to be evacuated tended to leave the city at night before the bombing started and then return again in the morning when the bombers had gone. During the Blitz of Plymouth in 1940 over 50,000 people left the city each night.

In all, around 1.5 million people moved around the country in search of safety. In the Rhondda valley alone some 33,500 evacuees from London, Cardiff and Bristol were found temporary shelter in the homes of local people. Life for the evacuees varied. A great deal depended on how well they got on with their host families and the local community. The local **billeting** officers had to try to sort out any problems that arose. It was not unusual to find whole schools being taken over by families who could not be found accommodation in local homes. Since most evacuees came from large towns and cities they were not used to living in the country. However, many city children, particularly those who came from the slums of the east end of London, found life in the country healthier.

SOURCE C

(above) King George VI and his wife Queen Elizabeth visiting Londoners sheltering in the London Underground, November 1940.

Rationing

The British government knew that the Germans would use the same tactics they had tried in the First World War to starve Britain into surrendering. The Germans knew that Britain had to import nearly 40 per cent of its food from abroad, so Hitler built up a large U-Boat submarine fleet which he used to sink British merchant ships. For the first three years of the war the U-Boats were very successful.

SUNDAY MONDAY TUESDAY WEDNESDAY THURSDAY FRIDAY SATURDAY

HAM, TOO

Half a coupon for a ham sandwich

But none for butter in a restaurant

WHEN BUTTER AND BACON ARE RATIONED, HAM WILL BE RATIONED, TOO.

The rations announced last night will probably begin on December 16. They will be a quarter of a pound each of butter and bacon for every individual. That means a pound of bacon and a pound of butter for a family of four.

Ham will be treated as part of the bacon ration; bacon coupons will have to be given up from your ration book when you buy ham.

Margarine will not be rationed. Nor will pork, sausages, meat, or any other food—yet.

There will be three kinds of ration books—a general one for men, women and children over six years old; a child's book for children under six; and a traveller's book for people who do not permanently live at home.

TRAVEL COUPONS

A traveller who is away from home for most of the week will have to carry a special ration book, and the coupons used will be deducted from his or her family's allowances.

If you eat meals in a restaurant every day you will get more than your ration in butter.

No coupon will be required for any butter provided at a meal in a café, hotel or restaurant, as a fairly normal supply of butter will be allowed to catering establishments.

Housewives will have to register with grocers to obtain butter, bacon and ham.

Officially a ham sandwich will be a meal. You will have to give up half a coupon for it, whether you eat it at a railway station buffet or a West End snack bar.

FACING REVOLT

If you buy a meal away from home which includes bacon or ham you must produce your ration book and allow the caterer to tear out part or the whole of a coupon, according to the size of the meal.

Mr. W. S. Morrison, the Food Minister, faces a revolt over his rationing plan, and he may yet have to postpone it until after Christmas.

Broadcasting last night he admitted that there was no great urgency for the rationing of butter and bacon.

He said there was no need for general food rationing at present: "I see no reason to expect any shortage of meat, and I do not see any reason why we should at present impose rationing.

"There are many unrationed things to take the place of bacon on our breakfast table," he declared. "To replace any deficiency of butter we must turn to margarine. There is no scarcity of fats. The margarine now on sale has the same vitamin qualities as butter. You may call them 'sunshine' qualities."

M.P.s are sharply criticising his statement in the Commons yesterday that there were no Government

BACK PAGE, COLUMN SIX

RATIONS The answers to your questions

? How big a ham sandwich can I get for half a bacon coupon?—A sandwich containing two ounces of ham.

? Can I order bread and butter or a roll and butter in a restaurant without giving up a coupon?—Yes.

? Can I get butter without a coupon at a staff canteen?—Yes, at all catering establishments.

? Are fried eggs and bacon or fried eggs and ham exempt?—No, you must give up a coupon for them if you order them in a restaurant.

? If bacon and ham are rationed, what about pork?—Pork is not rationed. Nor are pork sausages, pigs' trotters, liver, kidneys, chitterlings, and other offals.

? If I live in London, my wife and family (evacuated) in, say, Exeter, do we register with two grocers, and what amounts of butter and bacon do we get individually?—Yes, you register in London, your wife in Exeter, and the ration is four ounces of butter and four ounces of bacon a person a week.

? If butter is rationed what about margarine and lard?—You can buy as much margarine, lard and cooking fats as you require, without coupons.

? What was the British butter ration in the great war?—Rationing began on February 25, 1918. Each person was allowed four ounces of butter OR margarine a week.

? What is the German butter ration now?—Between three and four ounces a person a week—when they can get it.

And this is how far it goes—

Butter ration is a quarter of a pound weekly. That is enough, each day, to spread thinly five slices of bread—each four by three inches.

Here's your week's BACON

Bacon ration is a quarter of a pound a week. Four slices—each a tenth of an inch thick. Four-sevenths of a rasher a day. In the picture, *left*, is a side view of a ration rasher "life-size."

Treasure, 'spy' girl, found gassed

Daily Express Staff Reporter

A GIRL known as "Treasure," who is alleged to have said she was a German spy, was found dead yesterday in a flat in Alexandra-road, Kilburn, N.W.

She was to have given evidence today in a blackmail case at Birmingham. Her real name was Mrs. Mabel Muffett.

Lying by her side on a made-up bed on the floor was another dead girl named Williams, whose name was mentioned when the case openedp in Birmingham last week. Both girls were about twenty-two.

Both "Treasure" and Miss Williams were in their dressing-gowns. They had been dead several days, apparently from gas poisoning.

Police believe that as soon as "Treasure" returned from Birmingham, they decided to commit suicide together.

Constables forced their way into the flat after the landlady had noticed milk bottles accumulating outside.

A number of letters found in the flat have been handed to the coroner.

"Treasure" gave evidence in a

→ BACK PAGE COL. FOUR

DANGER-ZONE SCHOOLS AGAIN

SOME schools in evacuation areas are to be reopened. Mr. Kenneth Lindsay, Parliamentary Secretary to the Board of Education, said in the House of Commons yesterday that in many cases it may be necessary to work a double-shift system.—*Details on Page Seven.*

Rooms to let to view raids

"PEOPLE in South Queensferry are letting rooms for week-ends at high premiums to visitors who take them in the hope of seeing air raids over the Forth," said Major Monteith Carstairs at Lanark County Council's education committee meeting yesterday.

Staff chief is to leave War Office

Lieutenant-General Sir Ronald Adam, deputy-chief of the Imperial General Staff, is leaving the War Office to take up a command.

With Lord Gort and Lieutenant-General H. R. Pownall, Director of Military Operations and Intelligence, this means that the three most important General Staff officers—the Cabinet's chief advisers on military matters—have gone away within two months of the declaration of war.

Exit the infantry

A notice "We want a bicycle" was pinned outside a warden's post at Ilford, Essex. Soon afterwards two people each provided a machine. They will be used on patrol.

Finland shouts back at Stalin

'World will hear our reply today'

FINLAND answered back over the radio late last night to the "malicious attacks made on the Finnish State in Soviet broadcasts."

Speaking in Russian from a station near the frontier, the announcer said Finland could never agree to a pact such as Stalin has forced on smaller Baltic nations.

Finland's Foreign Minister, Dr. Erkko, also broadcast to the Finnish people and to the 100,000 Finnish Army on the frontier that Finland's independence was not for sale.

"Stalin's demands," he declared, "may be a small thing to a great nation like Russia, but to us they are very big indeed.

"A way can and must be found for Finland and Russia to live together, but no pressure can change our resolution. The country is determined to defend itself."

Neutrals bark

"When our answer to Russia is published tomorrow the world will know how far we have gone for peace."

[M. Paasikivi, Finnish Special Envoy, arrives with the reply in Moscow this morning.]

Sweden, Finland's closest neighbour, and other neutral States come out strongly this morning against the Russian demands.

After last night's meeting of the Swedish Foreign Affairs Committee it was stated in Stockholm at 1.30 a.m. that a Soviet naval base on the Finnish coast would be a grave threat to the Scandinavian countries.

Norway's Government newspaper Arbejder Bladet sees the Soviet claims as an ultimatum which renders further talk practically useless, and continues:—

"It is not the spirit of Lenin that marks Russian foreign policy but the spirit of Peter the Great."

A New York message early today says President Roosevelt has officially published the text of messages which passed between himself and the Kremlin as long ago as April. These messages indicate that Soviet Russia assured America she would not attack any smaller nation.

Russia buys rubber in U.S. for Nazis

Daily Express Staff Reporter

NEW YORK, Wednesday.—Despite warnings by President Roosevelt, Acting-Navy Secretary Edison and Assistant War Secretary Louis Johnson, the Soviet Union, through Amtorg, the Russian trading company, have bought up several thousand tons of rubber believed to be intended for Germany. Amtorg are said to be seeking 10,000 tons or more through New York jobbers.

That Man has "decided" again

'A QUIET WINTER'

MESSAGES from Berlin last night indicated that there will be no German attack on the Maginot Line until the Spring.

Hitler, it was said, has reluctantly abandoned his plan for a smashing frontal attack to restore German prestige.

The decision followed a day of anxiety for German army chiefs. Hitler, who has hardly left the Chancellery during the past two weeks, locked himself in his study and refused to see any one.

The Fuehrer broke his solitude only when he summoned his military chiefs suddenly for a one-hour conference at which huge-scale maps of the Western Front were inspected.

He studied detailed reports of the small-scale trial attacks on the French lines in the Moselle sector—attacks carefully staged by forces ranging from sixty to 1,000 men during the past few days under differing weather conditions.

Results of these trial attacks have convinced the German General Staff that a big-scale attack would be terribly costly.

It is expected that Hitler will now lay plans for a quiet winter on the war front and concentrate on new diplomatic moves to strengthen his position before the spring.

Tailpiece

While Hitler was planning a quiet winter for the troops, his own Nazi newspaper, Voelkischer Beobachter, was pressing on the nerve war—"Blitzkrieg for Britain."

The newspaper said yesterday:—

"Our proud young manhood are burning to deal those blows against Britain which are necessary finally to cure her of her presumptuousness, to put her back within the limits set for her by nature and her actual achievements."

** **Hitler turns hate on France, Page Two.**

SOURCE D

(right) The *Daily Express* explains the rationing system to its readers in November 1939.

In April 1941 alone over 700,000 tons of British shipping was sunk.

On the home front people were expected to make sacrifices in order to help beat the U-Boat threat. In January 1940 the government introduced food rationing, quickly followed by clothes, petrol and coal rationing. By 1942 even water was being rationed and people were allowed only 13 centimetres of water in their weekly bath! Ration books were issued to everyone and the ration coupons could be exchanged for goods like meat, eggs, butter and sugar only at shops where people had registered. Some foods such as bread, most vegetables and potatoes were not rationed. But fruits like bananas, oranges and lemons were almost impossible to get except on the black market, where most rationed items could be bought illegally for a high price.

The dog ran out of the butcher's shop with a large piece of suet in its mouth. I followed on my bicycle and saw the dog bury the suet. When the dog was safely away I went to the spot and [took] the hidden treasure. I took that suet home, cut out the mauled part and then made suet pudding.

SOURCE E

(left) One woman recalls how the shortage of food drove her to desperate measures in N. Longmate, *How We Lived Then* (1971).

Censorship and Propaganda

SOURCE F

(above) A poster issued by the Ministry of Information in 1940.

SOURCE G

(left) A poster issued by the Ministry of Information in 1940.

During times of war all governments try to control the news in order to conceal the truth. This is called censorship. In Britain as in Germany, radio, newspapers, magazines, cinema films and newsreels were censored. The Ministry of Information was set up to manage the rules on censorship and propaganda. The aim was to ensure that people only knew what the government wanted them to know or what it thought they should know. Military disasters were made to sound less serious than they actually were, as bad news was supposed to damage morale.

The government claimed that the censorship laws were there to protect people from lies, rumours and from German propaganda. During the war William Joyce, nicknamed Lord Haw-Haw because of his posh voice, was a pro-Nazi Irish/American who regularly broadcast to the British people from a radio station in Germany. His aim was to destroy British morale and the government considered censoring his broadcasts until they discovered that most people treated him as a joke. On the other hand, the *Daily Worker*, a pro-communist newspaper, was banned because it criticised the government and the war effort. Of course, good news like military victories and other successes were not censored but the truth of them was often exaggerated to make them look more than they were. This was propaganda. Both sides made great use of propaganda and this 'war of words' became an important weapon during the war.

Women and the War

An historian once said, 'It took a world war to give women freedom but two world wars to give them equality.' During the First World War women were given the opportunity to prove their worth as industrial and agricultural workers and their contribution to the war effort was praised by contemporaries. However, once the war came to an end so did their contribution to the industrial prosperity of Britain. Returning soldiers were given the jobs once done by women. With the outbreak of the Second World War the political leaders of Britain were in no doubt that they would be needed again. Thousands of women were recruited or conscripted for the war effort. They worked in factories making munitions, on the land growing food to feed the nation and in the hospitals tending to the sick and injured. In one munitions factory at Bridgend, 7,000 people were employed, over 65 per cent of them women.

SOURCE H

For the first time many women received the training to become skilled technicians and engineers. This woman welder is making machinery parts.

SOURCE I

A statement by Clement Atlee, Deputy Prime Minister, in 1942.

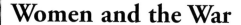

The work the women are performing in munitions factories has to be seen to be believed. Precision engineering jobs which a few years ago would have made a skilled [technician's] hair stand on end are performed with dead accuracy by girls who had no industrial experience.

Married women with children were not required to take a job. Women past their early forties were registered but never required to take work. Women over 40 were considered to be past it. The very idea of registering them aroused great opposition. But it was from these volunteers that the vast majority of munitions workers were recruited. They literally jumped at the idea of going into industry. They were emancipated. Freed from the grinding poverty of the 1930s, released from the kitchen sink, they had a life and money of their own.

SOURCE J

An extract from an interview in the 1980s with a woman who had been a clerk in a Welsh employment office during the war.

Thousands of women who want to volunteer find it difficult or impossible for them to undertake a war job. The most important reasons are: low wages, [lack of] day nurseries, long working hours and consequent shopping difficulties and [lack of] transport.

SOURCE K

A report sent to Churchill by the government's Labour Research Department in 1942.

In one factory the women are working from 8 a.m. to 5 p.m. There is a waiting list of nearly 300 and in ten weeks the bonus payment has increased, absenteeism [taking days off] has dropped and there are no fatigue [tiredness], shopping or transport problems, even though wages [£.2.20 weekly] are ridiculously low.

SOURCE L

'Women in War Work', a report published by the government in 1943 which was available to newspapers and the public.

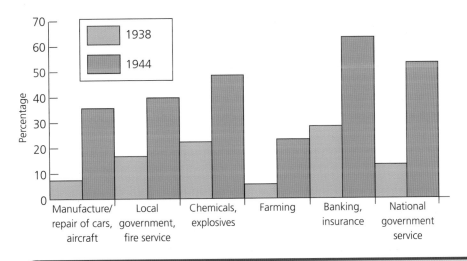

SOURCE M

A bar chart illustrating the percentage of workers who were women in 1938 and 1944.

?

1 **What problems might have been experienced by:**
   a) those who were evacuated?
   b) those who received evacuees?
   c) What were the benefits of evacuation?

2 **a) Why do you think the posters in source A were directed at mothers and not fathers?**
   b) How successful were these propaganda posters? (Use source B to help you.)

3 **a) Why was rationing necessary?**
   b) What were the effects of rationing?

4 **Why did the government report in source L present a different interpretation of women in war work to that of the Labour Research Department (source K)?**

5 **In 1917 an American politician said 'The first casualty of war is truth'. What was meant by this statement? Give examples from Britain during the Second World War.**

Winston Churchill

Early life

A photograph of Winston Churchill.

Winston Churchill was born into a life of wealth and privilege in 1874. In 1902 he entered politics as a Conservative MP but he later changed sides and joined the Liberals. He became friendly with Lloyd George and together they piloted many social reforms through Parliament.

The First World War

When war broke out in 1914 Churchill was put in charge of the Royal Navy as First Lord of the Admiralty. He proved to be an energetic and efficient First Lord but his plans for an attack on Turkey at Gallipoli ended in disaster. Churchill was blamed and he was forced to resign. Two years later the new Prime Minister, Lloyd George, brought Churchill back into the government as Minister of Munitions in 1917. Again he proved a worthy choice, working hard to speed up the supply of munitions to the front lines.

Wilderness Years

When Lloyd George fell from power in 1922 Churchill stayed on in the government, joining the Conservatives once more. By 1929 he had quarrelled with many members of his own party and he became an outspoken critic of government policy.

He was particularly keen to persuade the government and the people of Britain not to trust Stalin, Mussolini or Hitler. He believed that the policy of appeasement was a mistake that would eventually lead to war. However, few listened to his warnings about the dangers of communism, fascism and Nazism. The general public were afraid of the prospect of another war and preferred to believe in the peaceful foreign policy followed by MacDonald, Baldwin and Chamberlain. To them, Churchill's ideas about dealing with the likes of Hitler seemed aggressive and therefore bound to lead to war.

War and Honour

Churchill had been out of the government for over ten years by the time war broke out in September 1939. Chamberlain disliked the fact that Churchill's warnings had proved correct and he was determined not to have him in the government. However, the mood towards Churchill in the country and in Parliament had changed, so Chamberlain reluctantly agreed to him becoming First Lord of the Admiralty.

As the war progressed Churchill gained in confidence and prestige. With the attack on France in May 1940, and after a powerful speech by Lloyd George telling him he should go, and a vote of no confidence, Chamberlain resigned. Some MPs were in favour of his deputy Lord Halifax becoming Prime Minister but it was finally agreed that Churchill was probably best suited to lead the new coalition government.

Churchill proved to be an outstanding wartime leader. He set about restoring the battered morale of the British people by giving stirring speeches and by making personal appearances in various parts of the country to offer moral support when the Blitz was at its worst. Even when Britain suffered serious setbacks such as at Dunkirk in May 1940, defeat in the desert war in January 1941 and the fall of Singapore in February 1942, Churchill lifted the spirits of 'his' people by appearing firm in the belief that they would win the war.

His 'Drive to Victory' began at the battle of El Alamein in October 1942. Churchill's choice of General Montgomery to lead the British Army in North Africa proved successful. The Germans were decisively defeated at Alamein and again in Tunisia and Sicily. Churchill encouraged the Allied generals to invade Italy in July 1943 and France (D-Day) in June 1944. His hard work ensured that the Allied leaders – Roosevelt of the USA and Stalin of the USSR – remained united in order to defeat Hitler and Germany.

To the majority of the British people the Allied victory in 1945 was due largely to Churchill's inspired leadership. Yet he had his enemies. The Labour politician Aneurin Bevan criticised Churchill's leadership throughout the war. In July 1942 he criticised Churchill's failure to achieve victory and even called for a 'No Confidence' debate. In an attempt to cash in on his popularity, Churchill called an election in July 1945. He lost. He had badly misjudged the mood of the people. After a brief period as Prime Minister from 1951–5, Churchill retired. He died in 1965.

> You ask, what is our aim? I can answer in one word: Victory. Victory at all costs. Victory in spite of all terror. Victory, however long the road may be, for without victory there is no survival.

SOURCE A

An extract of Chuchill's first speech as Prime Minister, 13 May 1940.

SOURCE B

(below left) 'All behind you, Winston.' A cartoon by David Low (1940).

1 Did Winston Churchill's background and early career prepare him for the position of wartime Prime Minister?

2 Why was Churchill a success as a wartime Prime Minister?

3 Do you agree or disagree with the statement that Churchill would not have become so famous had it not been for the Second World War? Explain your answer fully.

OVERVIEW

Consider the following key question. How did people in Wales and England cope with the experiences of the Second World War?

POST-WAR WALES AND ENGLAND

The End of War, the End of Empire: Britain in 1945

> **KEY ISSUE:**
> *How and to what extent did the economic and social policies of the Labour governments change Wales and England in the period 1945–51?*

On 8 May 1945 Germany surrendered. The six-year European war was over. On 2 September Japan signed the surrender document that ended the four-year Asian-Pacific war. At the end of the Second World War the Allies – Britain, the USA and the USSR – emerged victorious. However, the British were to pay a heavy price for military victory. Six years of world war had brought economic decline and would contribute to the loss of its empire.

The Post-war Economy

The war had ruined the British economy. The country had spent almost £7,000 million, or a quarter of the national wealth, on the war effort. Factories that once built cars, fridges, cookers and vacuum cleaners had been used to produce tanks, guns, bullets and bombs. By the end of the war Britain was over £3,000 million in debt. In 1945 Britain may still have had the largest Navy in the world but could not afford to sail it!

The only combatant to emerge economically strong from the war was the USA. As soon as the war was over American factories were able to turn quickly from producing war materials to consumer goods. Unfortunately, war-damaged Britain could no longer compete. Its industries were unable to match the Americans for the speed of change or for the amount of consumer goods they produced.

Much of war-damaged Europe and the traditional overseas markets were in no state to buy British goods. It took American aid under the Marshall Plan to rebuild the shattered economies of Europe and so it was to America that these countries turned for support. However, America's wartime aid to Britain was stopped in August 1945.

From Empire to Commonwealth

Britain had been overtaken by the USA and the USSR who had become world superpowers. By 1945 American arms, troops and supplies vastly outweighed the British contribution to the Allied war effort. In the last stages of the war against Japan, between June and September 1945, British forces were given no choice but to accept American orders. It was also

American rather than British scientists who developed the first atomic bombs. These were dropped on the cities of Hiroshima and Nagasaki, forcing Japan to surrender.

Britain was militarily and economically weakened. In 1947 India, Britain's prize possession, was given independence. Soon other countries followed suit and the British Empire gradually came to an end. In its place the British government encouraged the idea, first used in 1931, of a Commonwealth of Nations made up of former colonies. Most countries like India remained a part of the Commonwealth but others such as Burma pulled out.

Yet despite the economic problems it was not all doom and gloom in post-war Britain. The country had won a war and there was full employment. The shipyards and coal mines were working to full capacity again and there was an air of expectation for a better future. Attitudes were changing. The majority of the British people did not want a return to pre-war depression and unemployment and they no longer cared as much as they once did about the Empire.

SOURCE A

The world enters the nuclear age, *Daily Express*, 7 August 1945.

DAILY EXPRESS

No. 14,094   Lighting-up: 9.39 pm to 4.33 am   TUESDAY AUGUST 7 1945   Weather: Cool, showers   One Penny

Smoke hides city 16 hours after greatest secret weapon strikes

THE BOMB THAT HAS CHANGED THE WORLD

Japs told 'Now quit'

THE Allies disclosed last night that they have used against Japan the most fearful device of war yet produced—an atomic bomb.

It was dropped at 20 minutes past midnight, London time, yesterday on the Japanese port and army base of Hiroshima, 190 miles west of Kobe.

The city was blotted out by a cloud of dust and smoke. Sixteen hours later reconnaissance pilots were still waiting for the cloud to lift to let them see what had happened.

The bomb was a last warning. Now leaflets will tell the Japanese what to expect unless their Government surrenders.

So great will be the devastation if they do not surrender that Allied land forces may be able to invade without opposition.

20,000 tons in golf ball

ONE atomic bomb has a destructive force equal to that of 20,000 tons of T.N.T., or five 1,000-plane raids. This terrific power is packed in a space of little more than golf ball size.

Experts estimate that the bomb can destroy anything on the surface in an area of at least two square miles—twice the size of the City of London.

When it was tested after being assembled in a farmhouse in the remote desert of New Mexico, a steel tower used for the experiment vaporised; two men standing nearly six miles away were blown down; blast effect was felt 300 miles away.

And, at Albuquerque, 120 miles away, a blind girl cried "What is that?" when the flash lighted the sky before the explosion could be heard.

In God's mercy we outran Germany

This statement was prepared by Mr. Churchill before he resigned, and was issued from Downing-street last night.

By WINSTON S. CHURCHILL

BY THE YEAR 1939 IT HAD BECOME WIDELY RECOGNISED AMONG SCIENTISTS OF MANY NATIONS THAT THE RELEASE OF ENERGY BY ATOMIC FISSION WAS A POSSIBILITY.

The problems which remained to be solved before this possibility could be turned into practical achievement were, however, manifold and immense; and few scientists would at that time have ventured to predict that an atomic bomb could be ready for use by 1945. Nevertheless, the potentialities of the project were so great that his Majesty's Government thought it right that research should be carried on in spite of the many competing claims on our scientific manpower.

At this stage the research was carried out mainly in our universities, principally Oxford,

The men who knew

SIR JOHN ANDERSON
He supervised the work

SIR CHARLES DARWIN
He was called in

PLANE KIDNAPS SCIENTIST

Snatched from Nazis to help us

A DANE who was smuggled into Britain and two

BLAST FELT 300 MILES FROM BOMB TEST

Steel tower turned to vapour

From C. V. R. THOMPSON: New York, Monday

THERE is reason to believe that the vital part of the atomic bomb with its almost incredible power of devastation is not much bigger than a golf ball.

We have not seen it; all that is given officially—and this from the War Department—is that it is "a revolutionary weapon destined to change war, or which may even be the instrumentality to end all wars."

But something is known about the first test, made in heavy rain at 5.30 a.m. on July 16 in a remote area of New Mexico.

We know that the blast was felt nearly 300 miles away. Imagine feeling in Piccadilly-circus the effect of a bomb dropped in Penzance.

And there is this account, given by the U.S. War Department, of what happened in New Mexico:

"At the appointed time there was a blinding flash, lighting up the whole area brighter than the

THANKS, BRITAIN

Says Professor

From GUY AUSTIN

LOS ANGELES, Monday. Professor R. Robert Oppenheimer, director of the work on the atomic bomb, told me

4.30 a.m. LATEST

1 What was Britain like in 1945?

2 Why might some people claim that Britain had little to celebrate at the end of the Second World War?

'A different Britain': The 1945 General Election

Two weeks after Germany's surrender in Europe the coalition government led by Winston Churchill broke up. Churchill did not want to end the coalition, but Clement Attlee, the leader of the Labour Party, refused to support him any longer. Attlee argued that the coalition government was a wartime arrangement which had done its job. The war had been won and it was now time to win the peace. Churchill resigned and called a general election for 5 July 1945.

The Election

The two main parties were the Conservatives led by Churchill and Labour led by Attlee. The Conservatives believed they would win because of Churchill's fame and popularity as the man who had won the war. Attlee was not so confident of victory but he believed that his party's promises of radical social and economic reforms would turn many people away from supporting the Conservatives. He was right. In order to allow the 5 million service men and women still abroad to vote, the election results were not announced until 26 July. Labour won a massive victory and it was returned to power with the largest majority in its history. As one historian put it, 'The people admired and cheered Churchill but voted against him.'

SOURCE A

The election results.

Labour	393 seats
Conservative	213
Liberal	12
Independents	22

SOURCE B

This cartoon appeared in the *News Chronicle* the day after Churchill resigned in May 1945.

Why did Labour Win?

The scale of Labour's victory surprised many people, including some of the party's own supporters. However, although Winston Churchill was hugely popular his party was not. Few could forget the depression, economic slump, unemployment and appeasement of pre-war Britain. Fewer still were willing to forgive the Conservative government which they blamed for many of the failures of the 1930s.

Many voters were voting for the first time and believed Labour was more likely to continue the spirit of wartime Britain where people had worked together for a common purpose. Many believed Labour would make their past sacrifices worthwhile.

Another reason for Labour's victory was the disastrous Tory election campaign. The Conservatives concentrated on Churchill's personality and war record. One campaign slogan said 'Help him finish the job'. However, the British people were keen to put the war behind them; they wanted to look forwards. Worse still was the disaster of Churchill's election broadcast of 4 June when he said that 'no socialist system can be established without a political police ... [Labour] would have to fall back on some form of Gestapo'. The pro-Conservative *Daily Express* newspaper printed the headline 'Gestapo in Britain if Socialists Win'. The British people were disgusted by this attempt to liken Labour to Hitler's secret police.

Churchill misjudged the mood of the people but Attlee did not. This was the first election for ten years and Attlee knew that attitudes had changed. He was also aware that people were hoping for a better and fairer Britain after the war. His party concentrated on a positive election campaign with the slogan 'Let us face the future together'. Labour promised jobs, fair wages, good houses, pensions for the old, free education and free medicine and health care. They also promised to rebuild the nation's economy and to return the country to prosperity. The British people were ready for this 'different Britain'.

SOURCE C

The front page headlines of *The Star*, 26 July 1945.

THURSDAY, JULY 26, 1945 *Latest Prices*   ELECTION RESULTS

THE STAR

No. 17,811 ★ ONE PENNY

A LABOUR LANDSLIDE

Caretaker Govt. Leaders Fall Like Ninepins

TORY PARTY CHAIRMAN IS DEFEATED: MORRISON, BEVIN AND CHURCHILL IN

"STAR" REPORTER

RESULTS declared so far in the General Election show that there has been a virtual landslide in favour of Labour, with gains from the Tories registered in all parts of the country.

Heads fell rapidly among the Churchill Caretaker Government. The first to be defeated was Mr. Harold MacMillan, the Air Minister, at Stockton-on-Tees.

In quick succession there followed : Mr. Brendan Bracken, First Lord ; Sir Walter Womersley, Pensions Minister ; Mr. Hore-Belisha, Minister of National Insurance ; Mr. Geoffrey Lloyd, Minister of Information ; Mr. Amery, Secretary for India ; Mr. Duncan Sandys,

STATE OF PARTIES

STATE of parties, compiled on the results declared up to the time of going to press, is as follows :—

GOVERNMENT

Conservative - - - -	62
National - - - -	1
Simonite - - - -	5
	68

OPPOSITION

Liberal - - - -	2
Labour - - - -	188
I L P - - - -	1
Communist - - - -	1
Common Wealth - - -	1
Independent - - - -	4
	197

In the last Parliament the state of Parties at the Dissolution was:—Government: 358 Con., 27 Simonite, 6 Nat. Lab., 4 National; total 395. Opposition: 163 Lab., 19 Lib., 3 Ind. Lab., 3 ILP, 3 Common Wealth, 2 Irish Nat. Abstentionist, 1 Communist, 18 Independent, 1 Scot Nat.; total 213. Seven seats were vacant.

GAINS & LOSSES

1 a) List the reasons for Labour's victory in the 1945 election.
   b) Explain the meaning of source B.

2 Labour's share of the vote was 47.8 per cent. This means that less than half the nation voted for a Labour government. How do you explain the newspaper headline in source C?

POST-WAR WALES AND ENGLAND

Post-war Reconstruction and the Labour Government

Having won the general election the new Labour government was faced with the task of fulfilling the promises it had made to the British people. In their turn, the British people expected a great deal from Labour. There was a general feeling that the country must not be allowed to 'fail' again as it did after 1918. The task facing Labour was enormous. Britain was suffering from the effects of bomb damage and this would have to be put right before they could begin to put their plans for social and economic reforms into action.

Bomb Damage

Britain's cities and large towns had been bombed during the war. The damage varied but the centres of some towns and cities like Swansea and Coventry were almost completely destroyed. Thousands of shops, factories, 20 per cent of schools and, most importantly, houses had been damaged or destroyed. These would need rebuilding. But it all cost money so the government decided to concentrate on the thousands of homeless people. In the meantime 563 army camps were opened to the public and used as temporary homes. In Kent the local council had nearly 1,300 homeless families but only 120 empty houses so it decided to hold a lottery: 1,300 people drew lots for the 120 houses.

  In its first year of government Labour built 22,000 houses and erected 41,000 temporary or **prefabricated** homes, known as prefabs. These were only meant to last for five years by which time it was thought there would be enough permanent homes available.

Demobilisation

In 1945 the British army, navy and air force had over 5 million men and women in their ranks. The vast majority had been conscripted to serve only for as long as the war lasted, and they now wanted to return home. **Demobilisation** was begun within months of the end of the war. Reducing the size of the armed forces would save the government money but, on the other hand, millions of ex-servicemen and women would need jobs and homes.

Shortages and Rationing

With the war over many people thought that rationing would also come to an end. Although the supply of most foods, raw materials and machinery improved, shortages of some foods like bread and potatoes, petrol, coal and clothes continued. Queueing became part of everyday life. In fact rationing for some items did not end until 1955!

(above) Men and women queue for coal at the Gas Light and Coke Company's depot in London in 1946. Each person was allowed 25 kilograms of coal per week.

Few complained about the shortages because they had been used to them during the war. The people knew that the improvements promised by the government would take some time to have an effect. They were willing to wait because they trusted the members of Clement Attlee's government to do the job. Men like Aneurin 'Nye' Bevan, the Minister for Health and Housing, Emanuel 'Manny' Shinwell, the Minister for Power and Coal, Ernest Bevin, the Foreign Secretary, Stafford Cripps, the Minister for Trade, Hugh Dalton, the Chancellor of the Exchequer and John Strachey, the Minister for Food were regarded as honest and hard working. Even during the worst of the hard winter weather of 1947 people were able to joke 'We starve with Strachey and shiver with Shinwell'. Although the Prime Minister Clement Attlee was a quiet, shy man he was a sincere and well-respected leader who managed to keep his promises to the people.

(left) Clement Attlee with his Foreign Secretary Ernest Bevin in 1945.

1 Why did the British people have such high hopes for the future in 1945?

2 List and, in each case, briefly outline the problems facing the Labour government in 1945.

UNIT 4

POST-WAR WALES AND ENGLAND

'From the cradle to the grave': Establishing the Welfare State

The Beveridge Report

In 1942 William Beveridge published a report which set out the kind of social reforms that he thought the government should carry out after the war. He pointed out that there were 'five evil giants' that had to be tackled by the government before it could properly care for its people. These 'giants' were 'Want, Disease, Ignorance, Squalor and Idleness'. His report called for a series of radical reforms to deal with each of these 'giants'.

Most parties held the same views about which problems faced Britain but

WHAT A MINISTRY OF SOCIAL SECURITY WOULD MEAN TO THE ORDINARY CITIZEN

Picture Post, March 6, 1943

What happens to-day to an individual who meets with misfortune : an extreme case to illustrate the maze through which Beveridge has pointed out a clear, simple way.

1 John Jones, a man of 64, finds that he has fallen out of work through no fault of his own.

2 He draws unemployment pay : at this point his case is dealt with by the Ministry of Labour.

3 After 26 weeks he is no longer entitled to the dole and is turned away to go elsewhere.

4 He has now to go to the Assistance Board. Here he applies for the unemployment help he needs.

5 The first of many investigators arrives at his home—this time from the Assistance Board.

6 He falls ill. Unable to work, he is no longer able to get help from the Assistance Board.

7 A new investigator arrives—from the Approved Society, which now deals with his case.

8 Still another investigator —from the local Public Assistance Committee, to which he has had to apply.

9 His 65th birthday present: a visit from a fourth investigator — to look into his pension claim

Wife Falls Ill — Son Steals — MEANWHILE — Child is Ill — All Mean More Investigators

A MINISTRY OF SOCIAL SECURITY WOULD COMBINE ALL THESE FUNCTIONS

John Jones when he falls out of work has plenty of trouble besides the gnawing anxiety about his family's welfare. He is passed from one set of officials to another until he feels like an official form worn out by constant stamping. How absurd that a fresh investigation has to worry him whenever he suffers a new misfortune, that there is no single set of papers about him and his family for everybody to consult ! When he comes to the end of his road—an old age pension—

he reaches the crowning absurdity: at this point his case actually comes under Customs and Excise! It is this state of affairs which a Ministry of Social Security would cure. John Jones would go to one local office for all his claims; there would be one set of papers about him and one investigator to help and advise. And the people working in this office would not treat him as a wrong-doer, but as a man fallen on evil times who must be lifted up again.

SOURCE A

A newspaper article from the *Picture Post* (1943). It shows what the Beveridge Report planned to do.

they differed on how to tackle them. The report was far too radical for Churchill but he reluctantly agreed to accept parts of it. His main aim was to win the war. However, his deputy in the war cabinet, the Labour leader Clement Attlee, praised the report and it was adopted as part of Labour Party policy. Most British people welcomed the report but there were some who opposed it. Many Conservatives thought the reforms would be too expensive and that ordinary people ought to be responsible for their own welfare. The pro-Conservative *Daily Telegraph* printed the headline 'Half-way along the road to Moscow'. It thought Beveridge's report was a blueprint for Russian-style communism. The pro-Labour *Daily Mirror* hit back with the headline 'Hands off the Beveridge Report'. It claimed the report was a blueprint for caring socialism.

> **I am all for educating the people into being less awful, less limited, less silly, and for spending lots of money on extended education; better paid teachers, but not for giving them everything for nothing, which they don't appreciate anyhow.**
>
> **Health, yes. Education yes. Old age pensions, yes I suppose so ... But not this form of charity [the Beveridge Report] which will make people fold their arms and feel that they need have no enterprise since everything will be provided for them. It is surely [an] error!**

SOURCE B

An extract from a letter written by Vita Sackville-West to her husband, a wealthy Conservative MP, in 1942.

Labour's Social Reforms

Once in power the Labour government set about attacking Beveridge's 'five evils'. They concentrated on providing income security, better health, education, housing and full employment. One of the government's ministers, Aneurin Bevan, was keen to emphasise Labour's commitment to establishing a system of family allowances and to setting up a free national health service. His vision was a nation that took care of its people 'from the cradle to the grave'.

THE BATTLE AGAINST WANT

In this battle the government concentrated on income security. In 1946 Attlee introduced the first of Labour's social reforms. Addressing a packed Parliament he announced the National Insurance Act. The Act provided benefits for the unemployed and pregnant women, pensions for the retired, and allowances for the sick, widowed and mothers with children. Later the same year the Industrial Injuries Act provided compensation for injured workers.

The minister responsible for the important Industrial Injuries Act was James Griffiths, MP for Llanelli, a talented Welshman and former miner from Betws near Ammanford. Griffiths followed this up in 1948 with the National Assistance Act. This provided the 'safety net' with which 'to assist persons ... without resources or whose resources must be supplemented'. The Poor Law and the workhouses were abolished and the Unemployment Assistance Boards of the 1930s scrapped. By 1949 just over 1 million people, mainly the old, were receiving assistance under this Act.

SOURCE C

On May 7 1945, the *Daily Mirror* printed an imaginary discussion between a British housewife and Sir William Beveridge. The following extract has been adapted from the newspaper article.

> **Housewife:** Do you think your plan will really go through?
> **Beveridge:** That depends on you. If you and your friends see that the people you put in Parliament want these proposals you'll get them. If you put in people who are against them – well, you won't.
> **Housewife:** Well, I've read about people who say they think social security is a fine thing, but who say we can't have it because the country can't afford it.
> **Beveridge:** It just isn't true. What is true is that we can't afford to do without it. A healthy, happy human being puts back into his country his own value. An unhealthy, half-fed person takes out from the community all the time.

THE BATTLE AGAINST SQUALOR

The Ministry of Town and Country Planning was responsible for ridding the country of squalor, or slum areas. In 1946 and 1949 two Housing Acts were passed which offered financial help to local authorities to rebuild towns and cities. As a result, between 1945 and 1951, 1.25 million permanent houses were built across Britain. The Acts set minimum standards for housing in an effort to rid the country of the awful slums that had affected pre-war Britain. The government also passed two Rent Control Acts in 1946 and 1949 which attempted to protect the interests of tenants against private landlords. Wealthy property owners were united against this Act.

Perhaps one of the most ambitious schemes to be launched by the government was the 1946 New Towns Act which was responsible for the construction of 14 new towns. Stevenage was one of the first. The government also recognised the importance of clean air and healthy exercise and in 1949 it passed the Access to the Countryside Act. This encouraged the general public to enjoy life outside the growing towns and cities. Country landowners were opposed to this Act which they saw as an invitation to trespass over their private property.

THE BATTLE AGAINST IDLENESS AND IGNORANCE

The Ministry of Labour was determined that people should never again experience mass unemployment. In 1948 the Employment and Training Act attempted to establish a skilled workforce. It gave funds for training school leavers and for re-training others for different forms of employment. People who lived in areas of previously high unemployment such as Wales were given the opportunity to become competitive in the world of work. By 1947 unemployment in Wales was registered at only 5.2 per cent or 44,000 people.

R.A. BUTLER

The man responsible for the reform of education was not a member of the 1945 Labour government. He was the Conservative MP R.A. Butler who was Minister for Education in Churchill's wartime coalition government.

government. He responded to the Beveridge Report by introducing the 1944 Education Act. By this Act he hoped to destroy ignorance by establishing free primary and secondary education and by offering every child 'diversity and equality of opportunity'. Unfortunately, he was never given the chance to fully implement the terms of the Act due to the war and the lack of money. In 1947 the Labour government passed the Act into law.

SOURCE D

(below) A cartoon by David Low (1942). An American reporter wrote: Sir William, possibly next to Mr Churchill, is the most popular figure in Britain today.

SOURCE E

(above) A cartoon from *Punch* (1947).

---

1 a) In what ways does the information in source A suggest that Beveridge's plan would improve the lives of ordinary people?
b) List the reasons Vita Sackville-West gives for opposing the Beveridge Report.
c) What reasons does the *Daily Mirror* give for supporting the Beveridge Report?

2 a) List the 'five evil giants' referred to in the Beveridge Report. Why did Beveridge use terms such as 'battles' to 'defeat' the 'evil giants'?
b) Describe the Labour government's 'battle' against the 'five evil giants'. (Refer also to the next chapter.)

The National Health Service

The National Health Service Act of 1946 is perhaps the best known of all Labour's social reforms. Its aim was to set up a health service that 'shall be free of charge' and available to everyone. This was a radical change. Although Lloyd George and the Liberal governments of 1906–14 had set up a free health service for insured workers, their wives and children had to pay for treatment. Visits to and from the doctor, medicine, spectacles and dental treatment all had to be paid for. For the many who could not afford medical care, their health, teeth and eyesight suffered. Some even died.

The Bill had its supporters as well as its critics but on 5 July 1948 its terms were put into practice. By 1949, 8.5 million people had received free dental treatment, 5.75 million pairs of glasses had been issued and some 187 million prescriptions had been written out. By 1951 only 1.5 per cent of the population remained outside the NHS. However, the service was expensive to run, costing around £355 million a year.

The Battle against Disease

SOURCE A

An extract from a speech by Aneurin Bevan, Minister for Health, in 1946.

> Medical treatment should be made available to rich and poor alike in accordance with medical need and no other criteria [factor]. Worry about money in a time of sickness [delays] recovery, apart from its unnecessary cruelty. The records show that it is the mother in the average family who suffers most from the absence of a full health service. In trying to balance her budget she puts her own needs last. No society can call itself civilised if a sick person is denied medical aid because of lack of [money]. The essence of a satisfactory health service is that the rich and poor are treated alike ...

SOURCE B

An extract from the *British Medical Journal* (1946).

> If the Bill is passed no patient or doctor will feel safe from interference by some ... regulation [rule]. The Minister's spies will be everywhere ...

SOURCE C

An extract from a report in the *Daily Sketch*, 1946.

> The Bill threatens the independence of the general practitioner [GP]. The doctors have a justifiable dread [fear] of becoming government servants.

SOURCE D

(right) This cartoon, published in the *Daily Mirror* in 1946, suggests that there was a small amount of opposition.

SOURCE E

(below) From a report in the *Daily Mail*, 1948.

On Monday morning you will wake in a New Britain, a state which takes over its citizens six months before they are born, providing care and free services for their birth, their schooling, sickness, workless days, widowhood and retirement. Finally, it helps [pay] the costs of their departure. All this, with free doctoring, dentistry and medicine – free bath chairs, too, if needed – for 4s. 11d. [25p] of your weekly pay packet.

SOURCE F

(above) 'It still tastes awful.' This cartoon from *Punch* (1948), shows the Minister for Health 'force feeding' the NHS to doctors.

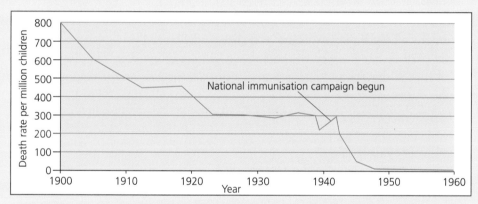

National immunisation campaign begun

SOURCE G

(left) A graph showing the number of children dying of diptheria.

The National Health Service, the creation of ... Aneurin Bevan, was especially popular here [in Wales]. It was popular even amongst Welsh doctors, with perhaps a stronger involvement in the local community than some [English doctors]. The Lancet [an official magazine for doctors] noted that a higher proportion of general practitioners in Wales (37 per cent) than in England agreed to operate under the Health Service in 1947 without waiting for the approval of the ... British Medical Association.

SOURCE H

(left) Kenneth Morgan, *Rebirth of a Nation: Wales 1880–1980* (1981).

1 a) How did Aneurin Bevan justify the setting up of the NHS?
b) Why did many doctors across the country oppose Labour's plans to set up the NHS?
c) Why were more doctors in Wales prepared to support the NHS?
d) Which publications (sources B to F) are *for,* and which are *against* the NHS? **Explain your choice.**

2 In 1948 a senior member of the Tory Party, R.A. Butler, stated that the Labour government had achieved 'the greatest social revolution in our history'. What did he mean by this?

Aneurin Bevan

A photograph of Aneurin Bevan.

Aneurin Bevan was born in Tredegar in Monmouthshire in 1897. His father was a miner. From an early age he showed himself to be a bright and capable boy. He was aware of the poverty around him and one incident in his childhood stood out in his memory. When one of his father's workmates had to have his leg cut off after an accident in the mine the local community rallied round to raise the money to buy a wooden leg. The miner's friends and neighbours organised a raffle and the young Aneurin was one of a number of local children who sold the raffle tickets. He left school at 13 to work in the mines, and as he grew up, he became interested in politics and joined the Labour Party.

At the age of 25 Bevan was elected a local councillor on the Tredegar District Council. By 1926 he was spokesman for the miners of South Wales during the General Strike, but as a result of the strike he was made redundant from the mine and suffered the humiliation of the Means Test. Around 11s. (55p) of his benefit was stopped because his sister was lucky enough to have a shop assistant's job that paid £2 per week!

In 1929 Bevan was elected the Labour MP for Ebbw Vale. He proved to be a superb speaker and talented politician. Yet his passion for helping the poor and needy and his outspoken attacks on those he accused of betraying the British working class won him few friends. He even quarrelled with members of his own party. However, friend and foe alike respected him. He died in 1960 aged 63.

SOURCE A

In 1951 a biographical profile of the Minister for Health appeared in *The Observer*. It was written to mark Bevan's resignation from the government. His resignation was due to the government's introduction of prescription charges for medicines. The following extracts have been adapted from the newspaper article.

Aneurin Bevan was born in 1897 in the mining town of Tredegar. The social setting in which [he grew up] was the South Wales coalfield before and during the First World War. It was the grimmest part of the United Kingdom, the part that felt itself the least connected with the war against the Germans ... the young Aneurin reject[ed] the ways of his father's generation. He felt he knew better what the real needs of his generation were, and that patriotism was not a useful emotion.

The only part of his father's ideas he agreed with was that expressed by the Tredegar Workingmen's Medical Aid Society (a miniature National Health Service). His father was one of its founders, and Aneurin fought his first battle with a local branch of the British Medical Association which opposed the rival medical aid society. The only ideas he accepted from Lloyd George were those of his National Insurance Act.

In the 'thirties he did not visit the countries threatened or seized by fascism ... but strengthened his position in Monmouthshire and spoke in the House of Commons on coal. He will not be remembered for his warning speeches against Hitler, but for his violent war–time attacks on Churchill. And, since the war, he has concentrated on ... issues [at home] – despite the crisis of the world.

Much the most solid and constructive effort of his political career is, of course, the establishment of the National Health Service. It is easy to see how his early training had equipped him to take on the doctors ... His driving motive was plain – his own experiences had given him ample [good] reason to believe in the need for a free medical service for the poor.

What is more surprising is his administrative success. He not only established the Health Service promptly, despite all obstacles, but earned the respect of his own civil servants. This may be the one episode in his career which justifies comparisons between him and Lloyd George.

SOURCE B

(below) The bronze statue of Aneurin Bevan erected by Cardiff City Council in the 1980s.

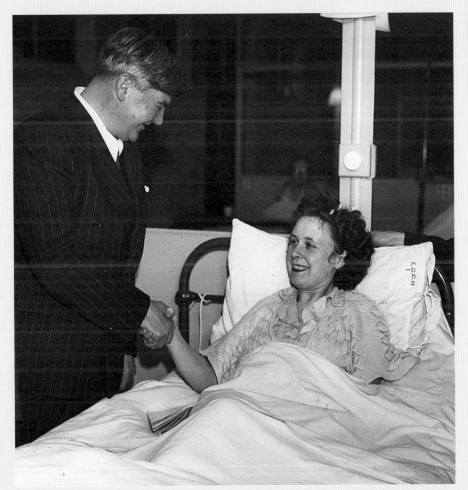

SOURCE C

(left) The Minister for Health pictured visiting an NHS hospital, 5 July 1948.

1 **What had caused Aneurin Bevan to be so passionate about helping the poor and needy?**

2 **Study source A and answer the following questions based upon it.**
   a) Why might Bevan have been called a traitor to his country?
   b) What do you learn about the character and attitude of Aneurin Bevan?
   c) In your opinion, is the writer of the article hostile or sympathetic towards Bevan? Explain your choice.

Interpretations of history

3 **What impression of Aneurin Bevan was the creator of the bronze statue trying to give?**

UNIT 4

Nationalisation

Socialists hoped that nationalisation would lead to a 'happier' people – the workers would feel a 'new' pride in 'their' industry and consumers would feel an equal pride in the industries which they 'owned'.
Profits made from state controlled industries would be used either to reduce taxation or to increase spending on welfare provision.

SOURCE A

(above) Peter Lane, *British History: 1750 to the Present Day* (1982).

Labour's commitment to economic change was as important as its social reforms. The government wanted to introduce radical measures to ensure that British industry would become more efficient and competitive. Attlee believed that the only way to achieve this aim was for the government to **nationalise** or take over all the key industries in Britain. These included coal, gas, electricity, transport, the airlines and iron and steel. He argued that some of these industries needed massive investment in order to modernise them.

The Labour Party supported nationalisation for other reasons. It had long believed that it was wrong for just a few owners and shareholders to profit from these key industries. They should provide good services for people rather than making profit. It also felt that the workers would prefer to be employed in state-run industries because they felt they would be working for the nation and themselves. Their rights would be protected by national guidelines guaranteed by the government.

In 1949 the Conservatives fought hard to prevent the Act for the nationalisation of iron and steel from going through Parliament. Although the Act was passed in the Commons, the Conservative majority in the House of Lords held up the Act for nearly a year.

The problems facing the government in trying to nationalise so many important industries can best be seen by looking at the coal industry. In 1947 there were 1,500 collieries in Britain owned by over 800 companies employing nearly 260,000 men. The government had to compensate these companies before taking over the collieries. The whole process was very complicated and expensive. With millions spent on compensation, millions more were spent on investment in new technology and machinery. Between 1948 and 1952 the government invested nearly £32 million in coal mines in the South Wales region alone.

In spite of opposition to nationalisation and the problems of compensation, the government controlled about 20 per cent of British industry by 1950.

The Bank of England	1946
The coal mines	1946
Cable and Wireless	1947
Electricity	1947
Transport	1948
Gas	1949
Iron and steel	1949

SOURCE B

The industries listed on the right were nationalised between 1946 and 1949.

For the Welsh miners and their families, nationalisation meant ... the reward for all the suffering endured from Black Friday [1926 General Strike] onwards. No tears were shed for the old private coalowners. With their record in regard to ... pit safety, and above all relations with their workers, they had few friends. Perhaps they did not deserve any. They [refused to allow] historians ... access to their [business] records in the National Library of Wales ... nationalisation ... helped promote a more thriving and harmonious [successful and peaceful] atmosphere in the Welsh industrial scene.

SOURCE C

(left) Adapted from *Rebirth of a Nation: Wales 1880–1980* (1981) by Kenneth Morgan.

SOURCE D

(above) Emmanual Shinwell, Minister for Fuel, is pictured on the left opening a newly nationalised pit.

COAL NATIONALISATION CELEBRATIONS

PROGRAMME OF EVENTS

Empire, Tonypandy Sunday, February 23. 1947

A SACRED CONCERT
GIVEN BY
The Williamstown Gleemen
The Tonypandy Ladies' Choir
Chairman: Mr. A. P. Glanville, J.P. Commence at 8 p.m. Silver Collection

WORKMEN'S HALL, FERNDALE
Sunday, February 23rd
A SACRED CONCERT
Given by The Pendyrus Male Choir
SUPPORTED BY LOCAL ARTISTES
Chairman: Ald. Alfred Evans, J.P., Mardy
Commencing at 5 p.m. Silver Collection

At THE DRILL HALL, PENTRE   Monday, February 24th, at 6 p.m.
The Official Opening of the Ministry of Fuel and Power
MINING AND FUEL EFFICIENCY EXHIBITION
By Mr. AERON G. THOMAS, *Vice-Chairman of the South Western Divisional Coal Board*
The exhibition will remain open until 8 p.m. on Monday, February 24th. It will remain open each day from 10 a.m. until 8 p.m. and will close at 8 p.m. on Friday, February 28th. ALMOST every aspect of life in the Rhondda will be covered by the activities planned for the week commencing February 23rd, and the exhibition will contain mining machinery, fuel efficiency demonstrations, coal derivatives, educational exhibits, Ministry of Food exhibits, Maesyrhaf arts and crafts, a Concordia display of miners' safety lamps, and many other items not yet listed.

WORKMEN'S HALL, TON PENTRE
SUNDAY, FEBRUARY 23rd
A SACRED CONCERT
GIVEN BY
MADAME DANFORD GEORGE'S LADIES' CHOIR
AND THE MORGANNWG GLEE PARTY
CONDUCTOR: D. LEKEY
SUPPORTED BY THE CORY WORKMEN'S BAND
Chairman: Captain D. G. Richards   Commencing 8 p.m.   Silver Collection

Polikoff's Ltd., Factory Canteen
A MANNEQUIN PARADE
Tuesday, Feb. 25th, at 6 and 7.30 p.m.   Admission 6d.
Park and Dare Hall   Wednesday, February 26th
A GRAND CONCERT BY
THE PARK AND DARE BAND
Supported by Local Artistes. Commence at 7.30 p.m.   Silver Collection

JUDGE'S HALL, TREALAW
Wednesday, February 26th
THE MAESYRHAF PLAYERS WILL PERFORM
"BIRD IN HAND"
By JOHN DRINKWATER
SILVER COLLECTION
Doors open at 6.30, to commence at 7 p.m.

Blaencwm Baptist Chapel, Tynewydd, Treherbert
Sunday, March 2nd, at 8 p.m.
A SACRED CONCERT
GIVEN BY THE
BLAENCWM CHORAL SOCIETY
Conductor: Mr. John Davies   Accompanist: Mrs. Janet Bennett
Chairman: C. Coun. W. Llewellyn   Silver Collection

CENTRAL HALL, TONYPANDY
Thursday, February 27th
A MASS MEETING
Speakers
General Sir Alfred Reade Goodwin Austin
Chairman: South Western Divisional Coal Board
Mr. George Thomas, M.P.
Chairman: Will John, M.P.
Music will be provided by the Williamstown Gleemen
COMMUNITY SINGING WILL BE LED BY MR. E. LLOYD ACCOMPANIED BY MRS. E. LLOYD, ORGANIST
MEETING WILL OPEN AT 7 P.M.

TRERHONDDA CHAPEL, FERNDALE
Friday, February 28th, at 7 p.m.
A MASS MEETING
SPEAKERS
Alderman GOMER EVANS
LABOUR DIRECTOR, SOUTH WESTERN DIVISIONAL COAL BOARD
GEORGE THOMAS, M.P.
Chairman: County Councillor T. Mardy James Evans
Music provided by
THE PENDYRUS MALE CHOIR

The proceeds of the foregoing activities will be devoted to Miners' rehabilitation ■ Fuller particulars can be seen in the Souvenir Programmes ■ JOIN IN THE CELEBRATIONS

SOURCE E

(left) A leaflet advertising events to celebrate the nationalisation of the coal industry (1947).

1 a) What do you understand by the term 'nationalisation'?
b) What did the Labour government aim to achieve through nationalisation?

2 a) Why was the nationalisation of the coal mines so popular in Wales?

b) Why did some coalowners deny historians access to their business and industrial records?
c) Analyse the information in source C. Does it suggest that Professor Kenneth Morgan thought Labour's policy of nationalisation was of benefit to the people of Wales?

'Set the people free': The Defeat of Labour

Labour's election victory in 1945 had been a huge surprise but their electoral defeat in 1951 was also a shock. Why? The tide had begun to turn against Labour in the 1950 election. Labour won that election but only just. Although there was still a great deal of support for Labour's plans to maintain or even to extend the Welfare State the public were simply not prepared to pay for it. Under Labour taxation had increased and it remained high in 1950–51. The Conservatives knew that no matter how worthy the cause, high taxes are never popular.

Middle-class voters were especially resentful at having to pay higher taxes. Although the war had been over for some time there was still rationing. Inflation was beginning to rise which caused prices to go up. There was a general feeling in the country that living standards had fallen under Labour.

Unfortunately for Labour the public's response to the policy of nationalisation was mixed. It was welcomed in South Wales and popular in the north of England but elsewhere the response was rather lukewarm. Many people believed that Labour had gone too far and that there was too much government interference in the running of the economy. Some were afraid that if Labour had another big election victory they might move from socialism to communism. The Conservatives played on this fear and they began to convince the middle classes to desert Labour.

The outbreak of the Korean War in 1950 made matters worse. The British government had to send an army to fight with the United Nations. This led to re-armament, which caused even higher taxes. The war was unpopular.

SOURCE A

British election results (1945–51).

	Conservatives	Labour	Liberals
1945	10 million votes (39.8% of votes) 213 seats	12 million votes (47.8% of votes) 393 seats	2.3 million votes (9% of votes) 12 seats
1950	12.5 million votes (4 3.3% of votes) 298 seats	13.3 million votes (46.5% of votes) 315 seats	2.6 million votes (9.1% of votes) 9 seats
1951	13.7 million votes (48% of votes) 321 seats	13.9 million votes (48.8% of votes) 295 seats	0.7 million votes (2.5 % of votes) 6 seats

After some six years in office the Labour government was exhausted. Some of its most talented members had either died (like Bevin) or retired (like Cripps). Others such as Bevan resigned because they were unhappy with some of the government's policies. In an effort to unite his party Attlee decided to call an election. It was a huge mistake. Under the slogan 'set the people free' from socialism the Conservatives swept to victory in 1951. Labour's dream appeared to be over.

SOURCE B

Posters used by Labour in the 1950–51 elections.

? 1 Study the election results in source A.
a) Convert the election statistics into a bar graph.
b) Judging from these statistics had Labour become more or less popular since 1945?

2 a) List the causes of Labour's defeat in the 1951 election.

b) Which of them contributed the most to Labour's defeat? Explain your choice.

3 Study Labour's election posters in source B.
a) In each case list what Labour claims to have done for the British people since 1945.
b) By looking back over the unit find evidence to support Labour's claim in each case.

OVERVIEW

Consider the following key question. How and to what extent did the economic and social policies of the Labour governments change Wales and England in the period 1945–51?

Glossary

abdicate – to resign from a throne or high office

appeasement – to calm or pacify someone by giving in

autocratic – governed by one person with unrestricted power

back bencher – a member of the House of Commons without a government post or responsibility

baroque – a highly decorated style of architecture originally used in the seventeenth and eighteenth centuries

billeting – to provide lodgings for homeless or displaced people

blackleg – a person who works during a strike

Blitz – the name given to air raids during the Second World War

Blitzkrieg – a German word for lightning war. A war of rapid movement

capitalism – an economic system that enables individuals to become wealthy or make a profit

coalition – a temporary alliance between two or more political parties

collective security – an alliance of nations bound together by a desire to protect themselves from an enemy

communism – a left-wing system in which there is no private ownership

conscription – a law forcing people to join the armed services in time of war

constituency – a district represented by an MP in the House of Commons

demilitarised – a place where no armed forces are allowed

demobilisation – to reduce the number of people in an armed force

democracy – a political system that allows its people freedom of choice to vote as they wish

dictatorship – a political system which does not allow its people freedom of choice to vote as they wish

dominion – a self-governing country within the British Empire but which continues to owe allegiance or loyalty to Britain

enfranchised – given the vote

evacuation – to remove people from danger to a place of safety

fascism – an extreme right-wing political system, supporting nationalism and against democracy, e.g. Nazi Germany and Italy under Mussolini

imperialism – the policy of extending a country's empire, its power or its influence

Kaiser – the German word for Emperor

Lib-Labs – elected MPs from, and representing, the working class in partnership with the Liberal Party

means test[ed] – an official enquiry to establish a person's neediness before financial help is given from public funds

munitions – weapons and materials of war

nationalise – to convert industries etc., from private to government ownership

non-conformist – refusal to conform to certain rules or regulations

pacifist – a person who does not believe in war or conflict of any kind

prefabricated – a term used to describe a building which is manufactured in sections and is ready for assembly on site

profiteer[ing] – the means of making excessive profits usually by illegal methods

propaganda – information spread by governments to persuade or influence public opinion

protectionism – a policy adopted by governments to protect trade or goods

radicalism – the holding of extreme political views

sanctions – action taken by a country or countries to punish a country or countries who break international laws or agreements

satirical – sarcastic, poking fun

socialism – a belief that the community as a whole should share in the profits of business rather than individuals

Suffragette – a woman seeking the right to vote through organised protest

tariff reform – changes in the duties or taxes imposed on imported goods

welfare state – a system of social welfare set up by a government to look after people in need e.g. the sick or unemployed